MARGINAL
WORTH

LIONEL S. LEWIS

MARGINAL WORTH

Teaching and the Academic Labor Market

Transaction Publishers

New Brunswick (U.S.A.) and London (U.K.)

Library of Congress Catalog Number: 96-6119
ISBN: 1-56000-263-8
Printed in the United States of America

Library of Congress Cataloging-in-Publication Data

Lewis, Lionel S. (Lionel Stanley)
 Marginal worth : teaching and the academic labor market / Lionel S. Lewis
  p. cm.
 Includes bibliographical references and index.
 ISBN 1-56000-263-8 (alk. paper)
 1. College teaching—United States. 2. Universities and colleges—United States—Research. 3. Universities and colleges—United States—Sociological aspects. I. Title.
LB2331.L477 1996
378.1'25—dc20   96-6119
                                                         CIP

Contents

Acknowledgments

I am indebted to the fifteen anonymous academic administrators and faculty members around the country who provided me with the many letters, reports, and other documents used in this book. I appreciate the useful suggestions of five friends who read most or all of the manuscript: Murray Brown, The State University of New York at Buffalo; Paul William Kingston, University of Virginia; Joel I. Nelson, University of Minnesota; Beth Anne Shelton, The University of Texas at Arlington; and Richard A. Wanner, University of Calgary. I would also like to thank Ms. Laurie Lanning for her help in the final preparation of the manuscript.

Finally, this book is dedicated to Jackson I. Cope: *"De Poeti, e Filosofi, amico e prottettore "*—and of a grateful student.

1

Introduction

It is a well-known fact that in American colleges and universities economic rewards (and prestige and power) are for the most part independent of any effort at teaching or putative success in the classroom. The salaries for faculty at institutions that place special emphasis on teaching are lower than those for faculty at institutions where both teaching and research are expected. Within institutions that value both teaching and research, greater rewards go to those who put their energies into research than to those who focus more on their teaching responsibilities. How reputedly good—or not so good—individuals are in the classroom has little effect on their salaries. The evidence collected and presented here suggests that this is the case because: teaching is not a particularly productive activity; its quality is not easy to measure; it does not generate prestige; most students do not learn a great deal; and in many instances, other matters absorb the attention of faculty.

Using concepts from economics, most particularly from the labor market model and sociology,[1] this book examines the contemporary academic labor market to elucidate why teaching, which is almost universally acknowledged both off and on campus to be at the center of American academic life, is not at the center of the academic labor market, and why it is only modestly rewarded. In short, it is an essay on salary determination in academia.

Given the culture of academic life where, for example, relative prestige is sometimes a paramount consideration in the assessment of individuals and their work, some of the commonly used assumptions of the neoclassical labor market model must be applied with caution. Nevertheless, a number of basic and too often overlooked concepts such as productivity and supply and demand prove useful in understanding how the academic labor market works, and why the return for teaching is not as great as many believe it should be. By way of example, prices and a system of prices can fruitfully be viewed in terms of supply and demand theory. Since salary is a price and the structure of salaries is a subsystem of prices,[2] a framework of supply and demand is used to advance the explanation of academic salaries.

In examining the academic labor market and teaching (and teachers), attention is necessarily given to assessing the effectiveness of college and university teaching and teachers and to the evaluation of the relative contributions of both teaching and scholarly and scientific research.

Academia under Siege

For several years and from all sides, American institutions of higher learning have been called to account for a variety of failures. The barrage has been uninterrupted, and at times tiresome and seemingly pointless. Assailing colleges and universities—most particularly the quality of teaching—has become a thriving industry, as there has been much with which to find fault. While some critics have been thoughtful and accurate—and conversations about faculty roles and rewards and teaching versus research have been heated, but heartfelt—many assaults have been politically motivated and mean spirited. A large number have simply been wrong.

Higher education has been on the defensive. It has had few champions, and their voices have often been drowned out by, among others, the full-mouthed clamor from administrative officers of distinguished colleges and universities and elsewhere, politicians of all stripes, executives of large philanthropic organizations, newspaper columnists, other opinion leaders, and an array of opportunists eager to see their names on op ed pages or for celebrity.

Interestingly enough, students, many of whom cannot find the requisite courses needed to graduate in the expected four years or who cannot find satisfactory employment upon graduation, have hardly raised their voices to complain. In fact, when asked to express an opinion, the majority of students generally speak highly of their courses and instructors, and about college life. For the most part, fast-track students do not select the most prestigious colleges or universities because of the quality of their teaching; indeed, many of these are precisely the institutions where it is said undergraduates are most likely to be ignored. They choose a school largely because of its reputation and the presumed cachet a particular degree will bring to their career prospects.

American institutions of higher learning, although perhaps a disappointment at home, are fairly well regarded around the world. American colleges and universities attract almost 400,000 foreign students a year, over sixty countries being represented by at least 1,000 students pursuing undergraduate or graduate degrees. In spite of these facts, higher education is still roundly condemned.

It cannot be denied that in recent years the higher learning has left itself open to attack. There have been scandals involving misspent research funds. Instances of scientific fraud are not uncommon. There have been too many documented and publicized cases of laziness and incompetency on the part of faculty. The federal government has charged some elite schools with collusion and price fixing. Athletic programs have been found in violation of relatively lenient recruitment practices and academic standards. There is the perennial accusation of waste and financial mismanagement. This list of complaints is long and one could readily expand upon it.

Significantly, the one indictment most often heard and that has found most support is that teaching in colleges and universities is not what it should be. There have been calls from all quarters for faculty to pay more attention to teaching—and to students, particularly undergraduates.

Within academia for most of this century, the reward system has been blamed for the neglect of teaching—and for a glut of uninspiring research. Consider these excerpts from the section on the relation of teaching to research in a report of the American Association of University Professors' Committee on College and University Teaching published in 1933:

"'College teaching can be improved by a decrease in the over-valuation of published research as the main measure of a teacher's worth' writes one successful college president. This assertion embodies an idea that is somewhat widely held in circles of collegiate administration. It betrays a feeling that many college professors devote too much time to research because college administrators over-value it as a measure of the teacher's service to the institution."

"Yet it is idle to profess any such solicitude for the good teacher when existing conditions are such that a man's [sic] success in research is everywhere rewarded as a matter of course, while success in teaching is not."

"When any young teacher, no matter where he may be located, makes a noteworthy contribution to one of the professional journals, he at once attracts the attention of men in the larger institutions. Presently he gets a call to some better post than the one that he is occupying, whereupon his own college, in order to hold him, counters with an advance in rank or salary. He becomes a full professor before his time. Hence the saying that 'research gets itself automatically rewarded.' But good teaching, no matter how good it may be, has no such advantage."

"Hence it is, also, that young scholars who desire to gain recognition as leaders of their profession are virtually driven to do research whether they want to or not."

"All this explains, in part at least, the considerable amount of indifferent research that is being turned out by men in academic circles."

"They know that while promotion will come in due course to the man who does his classroom work well, it arrives more expeditiously in the case of those who attract outside attention by their research work and their writings."

"For so long as that situation continues it is inevitable that research and other non-teaching activities will be used, more extensively than they ought to be, as the measure of a teacher's value to his college."[3]

The discussion about the quality of teaching has long been one-sided, and these charges sound as fresh as if they had been written in 1993. It seems almost besides the point that they in large part could be neutralized by simply stating that different types of academic institutions offer different educational experiences to students (as well as different occupational careers to faculty). It is not often that one finds this position in print. Henry Rosovsky, former dean of the Faculty of Arts and Sciences at Harvard University, is one of the handful in academia who have clearly articulated this perspective:

> [There is in] university colleges…the strong and sometimes controversial belief that research and teaching are complementary activities; that university-level teaching is difficult without the new ideas and inspirations provided by research; and that an ideal intellectual balance for the professor includes undergraduate and graduate instruction…. [S]ometimes, unfortunately, the behavior of a few university professors confirms the negative stereotypes: casually prepared lectures, office hours skipped, students snubbed, all in the name of some greater god called research. But

this can happen without the excuse of research.... A combination of teaching and research is part of the university faculty identity. The university professor is not a teacher who is expected to confine him-or herself to the transmission of received knowledge to generations of students. He or she is assumed to be a producer of new knowledge, frequently with the assistance of apprentice graduate students, who transmit state-of-the-art knowledge to students at all levels. The interaction of undergraduate student with college teacher and undergraduate student with university scholar is intellectually different, not better or worse, but different; in fact, better for some and worse for others.[4]

In spite of such perspicuous clarifications, over the last decade or so the faultfinding has become more broad-gauged and much more shrill and fulsome. The views of such visible critics as William J. Bennett, Allan Bloom, Charles J. Sykes, Page Smith, Bruce Wilshire, and Lynne V. Cheney, who have spoken and written with considerable ardor about the abysmal quality of higher education—especially the teaching of undergraduates—have been widely disseminated. On balance, there are relatively few defenders of higher education.

An oft-repeated charge is that the principle of tenure, which critics see as little more than a lifetime sinecure, has made faculty desultory. Too many teachers are burnt out yet refuse to retire, limiting the opportunities of those who can offer vigorous and inspired instruction. But unquestionably most commonly heard is the assertion that classrooms have been abandoned for laboratories and libraries where faculty pursue interests that are sure to further their careers. The charge is often made that the instruction of undergraduates—such as it is—has largely been left to inexperienced and harried junior faculty, temporary or part-time instructors, and graduate assistants. There is said to be a dangerous imbalance between teaching and research. The former has been deemphasized, and has become sort of a nuisance and distraction for most faculty who would much rather be writing books or articles, or jetting off to some conference. Teaching is ignored while research is venerated. In the words of Lynne Cheney, the former Chair of the National Endowment for the Humanities, students are victims of inattention "as a by-product of an emphasis on research."[5] Demonizing research faculty has become a national pastime.

Taking a historical perspective, George H. Douglas traces the demise of teaching (as the linchpin in providing a liberal education) to the founding in the late nineteenth century of new universities—the Johns Hopkins University, Clark University, the University of Chicago—that glorified graduate work and research over undergraduate education. Institutions of higher learning became balkanized, with individuals and departments at war with each other over funds and prestige.[6] According to Parsons and Platt, the development of a professional tradition and the growth of disciplines in the late nineteenth and early twentieth century made the focus on publications inevitable. Disciplinary associations served to communicate knowledge and as mechanisms of evaluation. Publications in professional journals became honorific and established reputations. The academic center of gravity moved from undergraduate teaching to professional concerns: "[P]ublication had a salient position, for publication was the surest way for a rising young scholar or scientist to become known.... Productivity became especially prominent, and the most tangible kind of productivity was in research communicated through publication."[7]

The attacks on the publishing scholar and scientist are unremitting and have even accelerated in spite of the fact that student/faculty ratios (at least at doctoral institutions) remained stable in the 1980s, at the same level, in fact, that they were in the late 1950s.[8] Even in respectable and mainstream periodicals researchers are insanely and unmercifully set upon. The following passage is worth quoting at length, as it so precisely typifies the thinking of the divers critics of the commitment to science and scholarship found on some—albeit a minority—American campuses:

The publishing imperative disparages the other major piece of professors' work, teaching; and it discourages critical inquiry into conditions of liberation of the self and of society. Further, normative concentration on publishing encourages us to ignore or reject, in academic work, the expression of the self's empathizing, nurturing, caring qualities and to sacrifice the self's delight in real connection with others. The publishing imperative requires us to forego what we learn from process in favor of the mandated alternatives of reification and quantification....Emphasis on publication, while effective in motivating some academics to work hard and to make valuable contributions to knowledge, can also stand in the way of useful inquiry, authenticity, and growth. The publishing imperative can corrupt the effort to take time in formulating and presenting one's thoughts, the style, often, of those who wish to write only when they are convinced they are ready to say, as best they can, something of consequence.... The pressure to publish belittles the struggle to identify issues worthy of study. It discourages the care and discipline required by the intricacies of growing which may include, but do not rest exclusively or primarily upon, written productivity. And it undermines dedication to the classroom, collegiality, and self-respect among professors whose talents lie more in teaching than in publishing or who choose the classroom, rather than the printed page, as the focus of their scholarship and epistemology. The academy's conventional emphasis on publishing caricatures productivity itself. By linking pay increases to publications, it encourages anxious deference to authority, ritualizes compulsivity, and mocks engaged teaching. In its insistence that scholars make their names known, the publishing mandate rewards excessive narcissism, denies the human centrality of relatedness, and serves unwittingly as a strategy for avoiding society and the self and their intricate interconnections. Careful examination of these functions might contribute to freedom from their odious effects.[9]

Apparently, at least, other factors are responsible for campus parking problems or that vending machines sometimes malfunction.

There is little question that research became increasingly emphasized on American campuses in the decades before the turn of the century. What is remarkable is that this is almost universally seen as having been done at a great cost to teaching—and is therefore an evil. Rosovsky would disagree: "Critics complain that teaching ability is ignored and that deadwood is encouraged to remain in place for many years. Without discussing these criticisms—and I do *not* agree with them...."[10] Yet, listen to Derek Bok the year after he retired as president of Harvard University:

> At one well-known university, my son, then an undergraduate senior, was recruited to teach a section of freshman economics to freshmen and a few sophomores. He had no teaching experience whatsoever; he was given no preparation of any kind; he was simply told where the room was and when the students met. "You're on your own," he heard, and so were his students, as far as that university was concerned.
>
> At many institutions, as we know, we have foreign graduate students teaching undergraduates even though they do not speak English well enough to be understood.

On the following page of his brief lamentation, Bok adds:

> And so teaching remains one of the few human activities that does not get demonstrably better from one generation to the next.... But we do not do a lot to improve what goes on within those courses—they are regarded as sacred territory. And we are not doing a lot to change our underlying priorities.[11]

Apparently a good number, even those who might prefer Mozart to John Cage, would agree.

What we are now hearing publicly and with regularity from college and university faculty is that teaching and research are "inescapably incompatible":

> [T]he present requirements for high-quality undergraduate education ultimately are incompatible with the sort of research programs now required to secure tenure, promotion, external support, and scholarly reputation and status.... Meeting students' needs will require not only a commitment to developing better curricula and teaching strategies, but also...the willingness to spend significantly more time with students. Such a commitment of time is irreconcilable with the demands of research

today, and, more important, is not valued in the professional culture of research-oriented faculty members. One cannot produce the quality or quantity of research needed to establish a significant reputation among peers as a part-time pursuit. So the research demands on individual faculty members will never leave enough time or energy for them to meet the need for devoted teaching and curriculum development.[12]

Such views are clearly more somber than Veblen's matter-of-fact, and to most, academics and nonacademics, anachronistic insistence that "the conservation and advancement of the higher learning involves two lines of work, distinct but closely bound together: (a) scientific and scholarly inquiry, and (b) the instruction of students. The former of these is primary and indispensable. It is this work of intellectual enterprise that gives its character to the university and marks it off from the lower schools."[13] And again, teaching is important "only in so far as it is incidental to an aggressive campaign of inquiry."[14]

There are corollaries to the variegated charges one hears on and off campus today: Faculty seem responsible to no one but themselves. There is little professorial accountability beyond relatively light and flexible teaching schedules. The professoriate is mostly free to do what it wishes, so that it can spend its time as it sees fit. There is little sense of institutional commitment; there is less sense of commitment to undergraduates. Where there was once a campus community held together by the need to educate undergraduates there is now anarchy. Academic life is no longer a calling, but a career.

Charles J. Sykes has gone as far as to make the assertion that "the academic culture is not merely indifferent to teaching, *it is actively hostile to it.* In the modern university, no act of good teaching goes unpunished."[15] Moreover, "in the academic culture, to be a good teacher is to be a failure. The indifference of the academic villages to teaching is readily understandable...the virulence of the hostility is more troublesome. The[re is] contempt for teaching and the professoriate's ill-concealed embarrassment in its presence."[16] Finally, "all of these permutations of lousy teaching reflect the academic culture's feeling that teaching well is simply not worth the effort or attention. In various ways they all reaffirm the subsidiary status of teaching: it is a job to get through with a minimum of time and intellectual investment."[17] The pummeling is unending.

No doubt, current attitudes toward teaching (and research) are rooted in graduate training and the graduate schools. The Ph.D. is a research degree. It certifies that individuals know anthropology or biology; it attests to their training as anthropologists or biologists, not that they have learned to teach the subject. The neophyte academic is guided step-by-step in completing a dissertation much as interns are supervised by experienced physicians. Teaching skills, such as they are, are picked up by trial and error or through having been a student. Seldom are they formally learned from a master teacher.

Even if it were granted that teaching was a neglected activity on American campuses, it would certainly not be sufficient, as many have advocated, to compel faculty to do more of it and to do it better. The problem, to the degree that there is a problem, is much more complex than simply restoring the balance between teaching and research. It is more than a case of the professoriate being remiss. Perhaps, after a protracted battle, in some instances a number of faculty could be pressed to have more contact hours with students; although getting more teaching from faculty may lessen a fiscal problem, it would not really deal with the question of the quality of instruction.

In the first place, certainly at least as central to colleges and universities as teaching and learning is the marketing of degrees. Learning simply for the pleasure of learning is not highly valued in student culture. The true reason most students enroll in educational programs is to get a diploma. Institutions of higher learning confer on those who earn degrees new social identities, a new status of being college graduates, which in the end may lead to favorable economic outcomes. Individuals are redefined by the college ritual; they are not generally transformed by their learning. College graduation has utilitarian consequences; a college degree generally helps one get a better job and earn more money. Learning as a result of better teaching may be of little practical value, of less value than simply having attended and graduated from college.

Few—even parents paying $25,000 or more a year for tuition, fees, and room and board for a son or daughter—would deny that certification is a central function of institutions of higher learning. To focus on what might be called progressive social transformation in order to make colleges and universities more effective or better places to learn, that is, to discuss reforms in teaching, is to disregard why the majority of students are there. As Randall Collins has pointedly observed, "the reason most students are in school is that they (or their parents on their behalf) want a decent job. This means that the reasons for going to school are extraneous to whatever goes on in the classroom."[18] For many students, college has little to do with teaching and learning, and a great deal to do with earning a degree and more money. At the same time, it is fairly obvious that colleges and universities are as interested in producing graduates as in learning. Students may not be interested in academic pursuits, but they are in short supply—most institutions need and seek out undergraduates who are not obvious embarrassments—and accommodations are made to indulge them.

Moreover, and more closely related to issues raised in this book, we cannot overlook the fact that the present status of teaching in institutions of higher learning goes well beyond teaching loads, efforts by faculty, and the like. It begins with the economic realities of contemporary American society, and is also closely related to academic culture and the academic labor market. In industrial-capitalist societies specialized competence, as shown through research, is as a rule more generously rewarded than general learning, by which teaching is often judged.

The chapters that follow analyze the relationship of many of these factors and the standing of teaching in American colleges and universities. The purpose here is neither to applaud nor condemn how rewards are distributed in institutions of higher learning. It is to show who is given what and, more importantly, why. The focal point is teaching, but the issues examined would be pretty much the same if it were research or service. It is teaching, as more academic do this than any other activity.

Although nearly everyone—academics and nonacademics—appears ready to debate questions relating to teaching, these are not any better understood than those relating to research, a topic that some will acknowledge they may not be prepared to discuss.

Wherever one turns, one reads or hears that faculty, particularly university faculty, should teach more, and that this would solve many problems. The following excerpts from a newspaper editorial[19] pretty well capture the most commonly voiced assumptions and arguments. The commentary titled "Can't Professors Teach More?" begins: "The main mission of colleges and universities is education of their students. That's a simple, well-recognized notion. It's why parents and students are willing to pay increasingly large amounts of money for the schools' services." Again, we see the questionable assertion that the education of students is the primary charge of institutions of higher learning, this time followed by a different non sequitur. Another paragraph declares: "As a consequence, many undergraduates find themselves being taught by graduate students instead of the tenured faculty. And when they do see professors standing before a class, they are rarely the big names that supposedly make the institution special." In order for this to be a valid charge, evidence would need to be found to show, among other things, that graduate students are in fact responsible for more than an insignificant proportion (beyond freshmen English composition) of undergraduate teaching (Is it in fact true that many undergraduate courses are taught by graduate students?), and that graduate students do not do as well in the classroom as senior faculty.

The piece continues: "As important as research is to the schools and— often—to the wider community, it should not be allowed to estrange the students from the faculty." How do we know that the fact that faculty are engaged in research contributes to student alienation? Perhaps institutional size is responsible for student drunkenness, cheating, and the like. Perhaps it is unrealistic expectations kindled by newspaper editorials. The critique concludes with a predictable bromide: "Additional ways to merge the separate worlds should be found, including more time in classrooms for research faculty. The principal mission should be to inspire students to learn, to inspire them on a journey to knowledge. A school that can do that has a lot to brag about, whether its faculty publishes any papers or not." There are many points that might be made here, the most obvious ones being that education is much more than teaching, and that it is unclear how taking researchers away from their work would merge teaching and research.

The materials gathered for this book should make it fairly obvious how useless—and even dangerous—such discourse is. It is glib, and adds little to further our understanding of the nuanced world of higher education and its reward system. There are so many ill-contrived notions about the higher learning abroad that a protracted examination of the place of teaching in the overall academic enterprise seems timely. In the end we should better understand how the disciplinary and institutional reward structures affect teaching, how and why faculty allocate their time as they do, and why teaching appears to be neglected and unappreciated.

Adam Smith on Teaching

Finding fault with college and university teaching and teachers is not something that began earlier in this century, nor is it uniquely American. Both have been constantly under attack for as long as schools and colleges have existed, and even before then. The fate of Socrates quickly comes to mind, but beyond mention of this, it would serve little purpose to recount the history of denunciations against schoolmasters and professors by men of letters, essayists, novelists, political figures, and students and parents. It is enough to remember that it exists.

Some attention, however, should be given to Adam Smith, as his criticisms and general observations of teaching made over 200 years ago fit together in a theoretical framework, and this makes them more than misplaced condemnation, simple carping, or random flashes of wit. His specific insights about teaching do not precisely explain the contemporary academic labor market in the United States. Yet, his ideas serve as a valuable model of how economic thought can be used to understand behavior in an institution that is presumedly not at the center of economic life, at least one whose success is ideally not measured in a profit or loss statement. There is no more appropriate way to precede the analysis that follows.

Smith's remarks about teaching are spearlike: "In the universities the youth neither are taught, nor always can find any proper means of being taught, the sciences, which it is the business of those incorporated bodies to teach."[20]

"In some of the richest and best endowed universities, the tutors content themselves with teaching a few unconnected shreds and parcels of this corrupted course [moral philosophy]; and even these they commonly teach very negligently and superficially."[21]

A major premise of Smith's commentary is that when the salaries of teaching faculty are independent of their success, they—as would be the case of individuals in any occupation—will not apply themselves. If they receive no honorary or fee from their students, it would be expected that they would neglect teaching or perform in as "careless and slovenly a manner" as "authority will permit."[22] Smith details why the behavior of teaching faculty is for quite obvious reasons often wanting:

> If the authority to which he is subject resides in the body corporate, the college, or university, of which he himself is a member, and in which the greater part of the other members are, like himself, persons who either are, or ought to be teachers; they are likely to make a common cause, to be all very indulgent to one another, and every man to consent that his neighbor may neglect his duty, provided he himself is allowed to neglect his own.

If the authority to which he is subject resides, not so much in the body corporate of which he is a member, as in some other extraneous persons, in the bishop of the diocese for example; in the governor of the province; or, perhaps, in some minister of state; it is not indeed in this case very likely that he will be suffered to neglect his duty altogether. All that such superiors, however, can force him to do, is to attend upon his pupils a certain number of hours, that is, to give a certain number of lectures in the week or in the year. What those lectures shall be, must still depend upon the diligence of the teacher; and that diligence is likely to be proportioned to the motives which he has for exerting it.[23]

These few sentences by Smith make it plain how comparatively un-formed and superficial the preponderance of recent observations about college and university teaching and teachers are. For example, in con-trast to Smith, an academic administrator, who is also a sociologist, has written: "Faculty also control their classroom activities. They may re-duce preparation time without constraint. Were the university a real com-munity, reduced performance would be controlled by communal norms."[24] Such scattershot generally masks as much as it reveals. In short, there has been much fulminating and even some cheerleading, but not much methodical analysis. As with the following example by an academic writing in an academic journal, too many pieces (even in pub-lications concerned with matters of higher education) begin or end with too little reflection or too little data: "Some part of salary increases— and ostensibly all progress toward promotion and tenure—are tied to evaluations of merit and productivity."[25] Many might wish that this state-ment were true, but there is simply no evidence to support it. The array of materials we have examined suggests that the truth is elsewhere. Fur-ther, there are so many institutions and disciplines that such generaliza-tions are perilous. What might be true at a research university, might not be true at a comprehensive college; what might be true at the fifty most select liberal arts colleges, might not be true at the 500 least select pub-lic two-year colleges.

Much that is written about higher education is unchallenged, although it is often unsubstantiated and off the mark. It is rarely put in a larger theoretical or empirical framework. Smith reminds us how much more fruitful it is to examine the question of the rewards for teaching and teachers in a context using both induction and deduction, as well as stubborn facts. There is some evidence, for example, that in the last few decades while there has been a growing emphasis on research in col-leges and less prestigious universities, a number of departments in some

top-ranked institutions have been making efforts—with some success—
to reverse this trend, to put a premium on teaching and reward it accordingly and to ease off on the pressure on faculty to compulsively publish.

Is the academic labor market enough like other labor markets so that
it can be understood in the same way they are? In the next chapter, this
question is examined by applying tenets of the neoclassical labor market model to the academic labor market. Chapter 3 looks at how central
teaching is to most academics in most institutions of higher learning.
The array of materials examined lead to the indisputable conclusion
that the academic profession is a teaching profession. Why, then, is teaching not given more substantial weight in the distribution of rewards in
academia? Chapter 4, considering this question, lays out the various
reasons why those who are said to make a contribution to higher education as teachers do not seem to be rewarded accordingly. Chapter 5 begins with a discussion of the negligible effects of teaching and teachers,
and concludes with an assessment of the work of researchers. In chapter
6 a close study is made of the deep-rooted concerns of faculty, and there
is little in the archival and other documents gathered and analyzed to
indicate that from the faculty's perspective teaching and undergraduates are very important in the flux of academic careers. Through an analysis of letters justifying merit salary awards, chapter 7 looks at how merit
is defined in academia. The focus is on the relative value placed on
teaching, research, administration, and service in determining merit, and,
while hardly overlooked, teaching is not always viewed as being as central to the academic role as are the other three activities. Chapter 8 continues this line of analysis using letters of recommendation written for
academics by other academics. Chapter 9 looks into how the academic
labor market actually works. Chapter 10 shows how academic administrators have contributed to diminishing faculty resources and morale.
The final chapter reviews the arguments of why the academic reward
system is as it is, and considers what might be done in light of motivation theory and the current academic marketplace to strike a better balance between expectations and circumstances.

It is an article of faith that when those allocating rewards give those
academics who are committed and effective teachers a fairer share, more
attention will be paid to the activity of teaching, and there will be a
noticeable improvement in instruction at the college level. The lament
that because work in the classroom is not adequately rewarded and as a

result is not as good as it might be is certainly seductive, but as it will soon become clear, it is a distraction from fully grasping why the academic labor market works as it does. But first it is necessary to see if propositions of the labor market model are applicable to furthering our understanding of the academic labor market.

Notes

1. Economic models of differential rewards generally focus on labor market conditions such as the supply and demand of labor that affect opportunities and the reward structure. On the other hand, sociological explanations emphasize the qualities of various activities and the individuals who perform them.
2. For economists, the theory of wages is merely "a special case" of the theory of commodity prices. As Hicks has put it: "The theory of the determination of wages in a free market is simply a special case of the general theory of value. Wages are the price of labour; and thus, in the absence of control, they are determined, like all prices, by supply and demand.... The demand for labour is only peculiar to this extent: that labour is a factor of production, and is thus demanded (as a general rule) not because the work to be done is desired for and by itself, but because it is to be used in the production of some other thing which is directly desired. Personal services are indeed an exception to this rule; but apart from this exception, the demand for labour is a derived demand, and the special properties of derived demand may thus reasonably be considered a part of the general theory of wages." [J. R. Hicks, *The Theory of Wages* (New York: Peter Smith, 1948), 1.]
3. "Report of the Committee on College and University Teaching," *American Association of University Professors Bulletin* XIX, section 2 (May 1933): 53–55.
4. Henry Rosovsky, *The University: An Owner's Manual* (New York: W. W. Norton, 1990), 84–86.
5. Lynne V. Cheney, *Tyrannical Machines: A Report on Educational Practices Gone Wrong and Our Best Hopes for Setting Them Right* (Washington, D.C.: National Endowment for the Humanities, 1990), 51.
6. George H. Douglas, *Education without Impact: How Our Universities Fail the Young* (New York: Carol Publishing Group, 1992).
7. Talcott Parsons and Gerald M. Platt, *The American University* (Cambridge, Massachusetts: Harvard University Press, 1973), 113. It is the professionalization of the academic profession, celebrated by so many, that Bruce Wilshire sees as the factor despoiling it: "The university is in crisis, and in significant part because of our proud professionalism" [Bruce Wilshire, *The Moral Collapse of the University* (Albany, New York: State University of New York Press, 1990), 95].
8. *Science and Technology in the Academic Enterprise: Status, Trends, and Issues,* A Discussion Paper (Washington, D.C.: National Academy Press, October 1989), 2–49.
9. Gordon Fellman, "On the Fetishism of Publications and the Secrets Thereof," *Academe* 81 (January/February 1995): 26–27.
10. Rosovsky, 32.
11. Derek Bok, "Reclaiming the Public Trust," *Change* 24 (July/August 1992): 12–19.
12. Bryan Barnett, "Teaching and Research Are Inescapably Incompatible," *Chronicle of Higher Education* (3 June 1992): A40.

13. Thorstein Veblen, *The Higher Learning in America* (New York: Hill and Wang, 1957), 12.
14. Ibid., 81.
15. Charles J. Sykes, *Profscam: Professors and the Demise of Higher Education* (Washington, D.C.: Regnery Gateway, 1988), 54.
16. Ibid., 58.
17. Ibid., 65. One can readily find many psychological explanations for ignoring students:

    > I don't think it far-fetched to hypothesize that some of the neglect of under-graduate students can be laid to their living in unwelcome intimacy with pro-fessors and polluting our pure intellects; that we load them unwittingly with our "projected" aversion to the messy, unruly, backward, and dirty body—particularly the underside of it; that they become scapegoats and are shunned. I think it is probably a case of veiled, self-deceived, passive aggression—along with whatever else it is. (Bruce Wilshire, 171)

18. Randall Collins, *The Credential Society: An Historical Sociology of Education and Stratification* (New York: Academic Press, 1979), 192.
19. "Can't Professors Teach More?," *The Buffalo News* (12 May 1995): C-2.
20. Adam Smith, *The Wealth of Nations* [New York: Random House (The Modern Library), 1937], 721.
21. Ibid., 727.
22. Ibid., 718.
23. Ibid.
24. Joan Huber, "Centennial Essay: Institutional Perspectives on Sociology," *American Journal of Sociology* 101 (July 1995): 199.
25. L. Billard, "A Different Path into Print," *Academe* 79 (May/June 1993): 28–29.

2

The Neoclassical Labor Market Model
and the Academic Marketplace

Although their purpose is not to make a profit, in a number of ways institutions of higher learning can be viewed as economic organizations. They are faced with problems of resource allocation and are subject to market discipline. Competition must be assessed and trends in demand must be analyzed. They also engage in advertising and product differentiation. In the end, decisions must be made as to how limited resources can best be spent in meeting an institution's goals. Still, before we borrow all or some of the conceptual framework economists utilize to describe the structure and function of labor markets, we need to know how typical the academic labor market is. In other words, is the academic labor market like other labor markets, or is it so unique that the standard theoretical concepts of economists are not applicable? With an eye to answering this question, this chapter examines how fitting or useful the neoclassical labor market model is in understanding the broad contours of the academic labor market.

Most simply, a labor market is the locus for the meeting of the supply and demand of labor services. In the academic labor market, the institution (the college or university) has a demand for services, which the professoriate supplies. Colleges and universities are the buyers and faculty are the sellers of labor. Faculty are presumedly engaged in the production of a capital good: trained and knowledgeable individuals for an increasingly complex economy.

An implication of the neoclassical labor market model is that the buyer (the firm or institution) offers remuneration consistent with the marginal value that services at a given level of skill will add to productivity. Given assumptions of perfect competition and market equilibrium, wages equal marginal productivity. The seller offers his or her services after considering both the range of costs that doing so involves and what will be given for them. In the determination of income (wages and salary), supply and demand operate to establish an equilibrium. Labor is attracted to those jobs that pay most. An excess of labor drives income down; when there are too few individuals to recruit for a job, the wages, or salary, will rise.

The neoclassical labor market model also assumes that both buyer and seller are informed and guided by economic rationality (self interest), and that the exchange takes place where supply and demand intersect. Other conditions on which it is based are that the units exchanged are generally monetary rewards and labor, that there is unrestricted movement, that complete information about market conditions exists, and that there is equality of power.

Labor markets do not operate in a vacuum, and are not perfect. The free movement of labor is often constrained by inertia; family and community ties keep many individuals from changing jobs. Union contracts may prevent employers from adjusting wages in light of changing supply and demand. Buyers often do not know where to find sellers; sellers often do not know where to find buyers.

The Operation of the Academic Labor Market

Since the academic labor market operates by a somewhat singular set of rules, it is obvious that there is not a perfect fit between it and some of the tenets of the neoclassical labor market model. Yet, the model can still be useful in furthering our understanding the academic labor market's structure and function. Even when appropriate, it must be used with caution. It is also worth noting that the neoclassical labor market model, like any model, does not fully and accurately reflect reality. For example, the labor market's function of bringing buyers and sellers together is always only partial and imperfect. In general, placements are mediated by information gotten from friends, acquaintances, or relatives or even by "blind" applications. Information about most jobs is not widespread. In effect, academic labor markets are internal labor markets.

With Regard to the Productivity, Prestige, and Satisfaction of Sellers

The first, and most obvious problem with fully embracing the neoclassical labor market model is that the productivity of the professoriate cannot always be easily determined or measured. A good deal of academic work—for example, that of an art historian or theoretical mathematician—produces outcomes that have no calculable price in the marketplace. The outcome and value of other activities, for example, much of what social scientists do, are mostly unclear. In industry, productivity and value in a labor market can often be readily determined.

The goals of most institutions of higher learning are also ambiguous: Should there be more or less emphasis on research? Should there be more or less attention to teaching practical skills? Is too little time given to the values (or the cognitive growth) of students? It is not always clear what colleges and universities are attempting to optimize, and the effectiveness of an individual (or an entire institution) is difficult to assess.

Moreover, prestige rather than economic reward is of paramount concern to sellers (and purchasers) in many exchanges in the academic labor market. The prestige of a hiring institution often figures prominently in the calculations of faculty seeking an academic position.

Another obvious noneconomic factor is the feeling of personal satisfaction academics might get from, for example, the amount of autonomy they are given. The degree to which one is able to chose the conditions of one's work is something academics often mention in explaining career decisions. Clearly, an academic's decision to accept or hold a job is also affected by other considerations, such as the amount of interest in one's work. Research by Marsh and Stafford suggests that because it may be inconsistent with their values, academics may forego pecuniary returns "for the sake of some compensatory substitute return."[1] In short, on the supply side the interests of faculty are clearly not restricted to only monetary rewards. But this is more or less true in the labor market as a whole.

Prestige Considerations of Buyers

At the same time, with regard to actions of buyers on the demand side, there is a neverending quest by institutions for more status; the shibboleth "pursuit of excellence" is often a euphemism for the pursuit of status. When hiring faculty, institutions commonly go to great lengths in their efforts to enhance or, at least, not to suffer a loss of prestige. As a rule, an institution will recruit from other institutions with a similar prestige ranking. As a consequence, for most individuals the academic labor market extends no further than institutions similar to those where they are located or from where they earned their Ph.D. Those with prestigious sponsors have an advantage over those with less prestigious sponsors. Because prestige is intruded in this way in the academic labor market, employers are not interchangeable, and faculty who might appear to be so, that is, those with essentially the same skills, are also not interchangeable.

Those institutions most actively engaged in the race to better their reputations often frantically court faculty who they believe will help them make their mark. They may eagerly pay generous salaries to attract those who they believe are prestigious. A key finding by Burke in her detailed study of the academic labor market of the 1980s was the reaffirmation of the conclusions of earlier research that the prestige system dominates the assessment of faculty in universities.[2]

Of course, prestige is largely subjective; in the assessment of young faculty it is little more than an opinion about promise. In essence, it is no more than what others might think about someone in the labor market; it is not necessarily associated with productivity. In short, what others think about a candidate can be as important as his or her actual qualities. Institutions, as a consequence, do not always seek or hire faculty who might add the most to productivity; they may instead seek or hire faculty who presumably would add the most to their prestige— those who appear to them to have the best academic pedigree, for example, a Yale graduate, a Brit, or a student of a Nobel prize recipient.

Is There a Single Academic Labor Market?

The academic labor market is not encompassing and can be subdivided according to the characteristics of buyers (i.e., type of institution—from community colleges to internationally renowned research universities) and of sellers (e.g., academic discipline). There is no academic profession; there are geographers and geologists, chemists and physicists. The academic labor market cannot properly be characterized as an occupational, industrial, or geographical labor market; it is much too segmented, and there is too little substitutability.

There is very little overlap in the labor market for universities and the labor market for colleges. For the former, sellers are expected to have an interest in or potential for research; such a capacity is hardly a consideration for the latter. There is a market for junior faculty and a market for senior faculty, each operating in a distinct manner. As suggested, new Ph.D.s can realistically aspire only for openings in departments at or below the prestige level of the one from which they earned their degree. On the other hand, positions are sometimes created for prominent scholars or scientists who make it known that they would be interested in or willing to move.

Moreover, the markets for each discipline may be quite different. In 1991, when the employment prospects for those attempting to launch an academic career were generally poor, the American Council on Education reported that for the previous year there were faculty shortages in computer sciences (46 percent of institutions), business (39 percent of institutions), health professions (37 percent of institutions), and mathematics (30 percent of institutions). The survey found that "in each of these areas, the percentage of institutions unable to find qualified persons for vacant positions has increased since 1989."[3]

These figures seem hardly believable and are clearly somewhat exaggerated[4]; however, other data do support the contention that there is not one academic labor market, but many. A study of 1992–93 academic salaries shows that the average salary for newly hired assistant professors in marketing was $50,000, while newly hired assistant professors in political science, where there are fewer market options, earned an average of $32,000. At public institutions, a new assistant professor of accounting earned an average salary of $50,723, while one in history earned $31,515. With the exception of full professors at private institutions, for each rank, computer scientists earned more than physicists.[5] This is hardly surprising in light of a 1992 survey by the American Institute of Physics, which found that the number of job openings for doctoral-level physicists at universities, national laboratories, and industry was about 800, while the number of Ph.D.s awarded in the discipline that year was 1,350.[6]

While computer scientists continue to be in demand (on and off campus), the number of openings advertised for 1992–93 in English departments in the Modern Language Association's *Job Information List* was 45 percent lower than in 1988–89. In fact, the number of positions advertised in 1992–93 was lower than during the 1977–79 period, the previous low point in hiring English faculty. In 1988–89, there were 2,146 positions advertised; in 1992–93, there were 1,188 advertised.[7]

The job market for sociology also appears to be sluggish. There were 1,161 jobs advertised in the American Sociological Association's *Employment Bulletin* in 1990; this figure declined to 970 in 1991. There were only 585 nonduplicate advertisements placed by academic institutions (plus seventy-four for sociological practice and postdoctoral fellowships) from July, 1991 through June, 1992. [8]

In addition, it would appear that submarkets are much narrower than any given discipline. Departments that expect faculty members to publish or enhance their visibility will not consider an individual who is unlikely to do so. Those who teach and those who teach and do research are distinct labor pools, and are insulated from one another by separate career ladders. With distinct career lines, their activities are noncompeting. Faculty with degrees from second- or third-tier institutions are unlikely to pursue openings (if they even know about them) in prestigious departments, and if they do, they are unlikely to receive serious attention. Finally, the specialized subdisciplines within a department—which may or may not want another theorist or an algebraist—are likely to define the market. In sum, there are different reward and status trajectories. There is labor market segmentation. Salaries are higher not only for faculty in disciplines whose graduates have greater earning power, but also for faculty at institutions whose undergraduates have the highest occupational and economic attainment.

Donald Light goes as far as to contend that the academic profession "does not exist," that the academic man (or woman) "is a myth." His argument is that while scholarship and science, which serve to advance knowledge, have the basic attributes of a profession, such as the power to recruit and train new members and the right to certify who is ultimately qualified, the activities of setting standards center on each discipline. What exists, Light claims, are academic professions, one for each discipline: "Each discipline has its own history, its own intellectual style, a distinct sense of timing, different preferences for articles and books, and different career lines which shift as segments of the profession alter."[9] Furthermore, the concept of a single academic profession ignores some in the scholarly and scientific profession who do not work in institutions of higher learning and bonds they may have with some who do. Light's position is quite persuasive.

Other Considerations

In the academic hiring process there is not complete knowledge; on the contrary, there are large gaps in what departments and those seeking and finding positions know about each other. There is asymmetric information. It is worth adding that, because those who hold market power can alter rewards and other employment conditions, in a buyer's market departments and institutions have an inordinate amount of power, and in a seller's market the balance is reversed.

All of this suggests that when using concepts of the neoclassical labor market model, which at times can be quite suitable and useful, one must proceed with considerable caution when they are employed to describe the academic labor market. An uncritical acceptance and application of the neoclassical labor market model do not enable one to understand a number of subtleties and singular features of the academic labor market. With these caveats in mind, we will proceed.

The State of the Academic Labor Market

For most of the twentieth century and certainly since World War II, with the exception of the 1960s, the academic marketplace has favored buyers rather than sellers. In academia in the 1960s there was explosive growth, limitless opportunities for some, and a great deal of movement, but these years were not typical. For the last two decades, much of the academic labor market could be accurately described as inert. Economic conditions have been at a standstill. Between 1971 and 1992 average real academic salaries (salary growth adjusted for inflation) decreased from slightly over $50,000 to about $46,000. There was a significant decrease between and 1973 and 1981 when average real salaries declined to $40,000, some recovery during most of the 1980s, and general stagnation between 1987 and 1993. Real salaries declined in ten of those twenty-one years. The most recent data on hand show that between the 1991–92 and 1992–93 academic years nominal salaries rose 2.5 percent; after adjusting for inflation, however, real salaries declined by .4 percent.[10]

There have been predictions that the academic labor market will get better in the near term as the aging professoriate begins to retire in large numbers; we will have to wait and see if this happens. A large-scale survey of 480 institutions of higher learning conducted from December, 1987 through October, 1988 by the National Center for Educational Statistics indicated a relatively static academic labor market at that time:

Between the 1986 and 1987 fall terms, the number of full-time faculty increased by .5 percent. The same number (39 percent) of institutions increased as decreased the size of their faculty.

There was an increase of tenured faculty of 1.0 percent. 53 percent of the institutions reported an increase in tenured faculty and 32 percent reported a decrease.

The number of full-time faculty hired during the 1986–87 academic year was equivalent to 7.5 percent of faculty during the 1986 fall term (7.0 percent of the faculty having departed).

During the year, 1.8 percent of the faculty retired. This number was 55 percent of all departures of tenured faculty. (Another 33 percent of tenured faculty who departed assumed another position.)[11]

In the early 1990s the academic labor market remained relatively quiescent. At the same time, the standard of living of the professoriate, which improved markedly in the 1960s before falling back, then stabilizing, began once more to erode.

What has been described is not an ideal environment for faculty, whatever their contributions, to be rewarded for their efforts. It is not a situation that will necessarily enhance their motivation. The prospects for most are bleak, and those who concentrate only on teaching are least likely to find a better academic placement. As will become evident, faculty committed only to teaching are disadvantaged in the search for an academic position or in an attempt to move from one institution to another. To the degree that this is true, it would appear that in effect the academic marketplace discriminates against most academics.[12] For, as chapter 3 makes quite apparent, the principal occupation of the higher learning in America is teaching.

Notes

1. John F. Marsh, Jr. and Frank P. Stafford, "The Effects of Values on Pecuniary Behavior: The Case of Academicians," *American Sociological Review* 32 (October 1967): 747.
2. Dolores L. Burke, *A New Academic Marketplace* (Westport, Conn.: Greenwood Press, 1988).
3. Elaine El-Khawas, *Campus Trends, 1991* [Higher Education Panel Report (Washington, D. C.: American Council on Education, 1991)], vi.
4. A more recent survey by the American Mathematical Society and the Mathematical Association of America found that the unemployment rate for 1992 Ph.D. recipients was 12.7 percent, the highest level since 1975. The total number of new Ph.D.s who found employment in the United States declined by 8 percent between 1991 and 1992. [Edward R. Silverman, "Recession Subtracting Much, Adding Little to Fortunes of New Math Ph.D.s Who Teach," *The Scientist* 7 (3 May 1993): 19.] These figures are consistent with what is reported in the media: "Last year, 12.4 percent of new math Ph.D.s—the highest level ever measured—had no job after graduation; the rate was 4 percent in 1981" [*Newsweek* (5 December 1994), 62].

5. Denise K. Magner, "Engineering Professors Hold on to Top Spot in Survey of Campus Salaries for 1992-93," *Chronicle of Higher Education* (31 March 1993): A14-A16.

6. Malcolm W. Browne, "End of Cold War Clouds Research as Openings in Science Dwindle," *New York Times* (20 February 1994): 1 and 36. In 1993, the situation was apparently no better: "Among new physics grads, 12 percent of Ph.D.s were unemployed last year," and "2.4 percent of physicists were jobless last year, up from 1.5 percent the year before" [*Newsweek* (5 December 1994): 62].

7. "Downturn in *Job Information List* Advertisements Continues in 1992-93," *MLA Newsletter* 25 (Summer 1993): 1-2.

8. Dan Clawson and Kathleen Holmes, "The Job Market in Sociology," *Footnotes* 20 (November 1992): 7.

9. Donald Light, Jr., "Introduction: The Structure of the Academic Professions," *Sociology of Education* 47 (Winter 1964): 12.

10. "Treading Water: The Annual Report of the Economic Status of the Profession, 1992-93," *Academe* 79 (March/April 1993): 8-10.

11. "Institutional Policies and Practices regarding Faculty in Higher Education," 1988 National Survey of Postsecondary Faculty, (U.S. Department of Education, Office of Educational Research and Improvement, January 1990), section 3. Predicting the number of faculty positions that will be open in the short- or long-term is perilous. In 1994, with generous incentives, the University of California induced 941 faculty to take early retirement, bringing the number to 1,996 who have done so since 1990. The larger figure is about 20 percent of the nine-campus university's permanent faculty. This does not mean all of these vacancies will be filled, even with junior faculty at much lower salaries.

12. The vice president for academic affairs and provost of the University of Oregon has proposed creating teaching professorships at research universities. In this way, "high-quality teaching" would be rewarded. The long-term effect would be to change academic culture, in that faculty would focus as much on teaching as on research. Most important, given such opportunities for mobility, teaching faculty would no longer be excluded from the academic marketplace. (Unfortunately, this argument rests on a number of questionable assumptions: that research universities should respond to the public perception that undergraduates are neglected even if it is false; that undergraduates are neglected because faculty are too heavily involved in research; that faculty pay more attention to research than teaching; that it is academic culture and not economic principles that exclude those who focus solely on teaching from the academic labor market; that rewarding "high-quality teaching" would improve undergraduate teaching; that undergraduate teaching needs to be improved; that undergraduate teaching can be improved; that rewarding a small number of teachers will significantly improve the quality of undergraduate teaching; that one can be an effective teacher in a university without being a successful scholar or scientist; that such a plan would result in students becoming better educated and more satisfied.) [Norman K. Wessells, "Using Job Mobility to Reward Good Teaching," *Chronicle of Higher Education* (27 July 1994): B3].

3

Academics as Teachers

Teaching, what most faculty are hired to do and what most do most of the time, does not figure prominently in the academic labor market. This condition prevails in spite of the fact that the American academic profession is a teaching profession.

American institutions of higher learning were from the first designed for undergraduate instruction. Faculty work load is calculated largely in terms of hours of formal instruction. It is expected that undergraduates learn something from their professors, and the assessment of students and teachers is primarily determined by what goes on in the classroom. (Students in France or England, on the other hand, are judged solely on the outcome of examinations.) Teaching is the nearest thing to a common activity of the academic profession; although their research styles and interests might greatly differ, humanists, scientists, social scientists, and those in the professional schools all teach. It is the defining academic activity. Teaching is the work for which faculty are paid; the demand for instruction is what creates almost all academic jobs, but as is evident, not the academic labor market. It is somewhat of a paradox that teaching is central to most of the professoriate, but not for the minority who are most likely to participate in the academic labor market, and are defined by their research.

By inclination and deed the vast majority of American academics are teachers rather than researchers. An overwhelming number prefer teaching to research. Even in universities, where faculty are expected to devote a substantial amount of their time to research and publication, there seems to be more attention to and interest and involvement in teaching than is commonly believed.[1] In every way possible, American academics affirm the centrality of teaching to the academic role.

Most academics work in institutions in which teaching is their primary responsibility. Overall, American academics spend approximately three times as much of their time teaching as doing research; many spend almost all of their work time teaching. One recent U. S. Department of Education survey found that for full-time faculty the teaching/research ratio for men was 54 percent to 18 percent; for women it was 61 percent to 12 percent. Even at prestigious, private research universities faculty spend more time teaching than doing research.[2] Half of American academics spend four or fewer hours a week involved in research not related to their teaching.[3]

At the same time, the teaching load at almost three-fourths of institutions of higher learning is four or more courses a semester. At almost 80 percent of two-year institutions faculty teach ten or more courses a year. At 55 percent of four-year colleges, faculty teach eight or more courses a year. About the same percent of independent institutions assign faculty eight or more courses a year.[4]

With regularity, national surveys of the American professoriate show that many more identify themselves as teachers than as researchers. About twice as many (between four and five out of ten) prefer the term *teacher* to describe themselves than the terms *scholar* and *scientist* combined. Only a handful, almost all from top-rated institutions, believe that the term *teacher* does not accurately describe them.[5]

When asked about various academic responsibilities, four in ten faculty report that they are primarily interested in teaching, which is about seven times the number primarily interested in research. The rest are equally interested in teaching and research, with slightly more claiming a preference for the former over the latter. In four-year institutions about a quarter of the faculty say that their interests lie primarily in teaching and about a third lean toward teaching; the interests of about one in ten lie primarily in research and about a third lean toward research. Even in research institutions a third or more of the faculty say their interests lie primarily or lean toward teaching. At research and doctoral granting universities about as many faculty are interested primarily in teaching as in research; even in these types of institutions close to three in four are almost equally interested in both.[6]

One-third of the professoriate spends more than twelve hours a week teaching classes, while another one-third spends less than nine hours a week teaching classes. Teaching loads vary considerably, and it hardly needs to be pointed out that the type of institution where one holds an appointment in large part determines how many courses a term one is expected to teach. At research universities, nearly two-thirds of the faculty spend five or fewer hours a week in formal undergraduate instruction. At comprehensive colleges, only one in five faculty spend that little time with undergraduates. At two-year colleges, four of five faculty are in the classroom eleven or more hours a week; the figure is two of five at comprehensive colleges and less than one of ten at research universities. (The reverse pattern is true for time spent doing research: One-fourth of the professoriate spends twelve or more hours a week engaged in research and an almost equal number does no research. At universities, only a handful of faculty are not engaged in scholarship unrelated to teaching; at two-year colleges, only a handful spend twelve or more hours a week conducting research unrelated to teaching responsibilities.)

The Minnesota College Teacher Study found that in four-year institutions the median percentages of time spent by faculty in teaching and activities related to teaching—preparing materials, grading papers, advising students, and the like—were 64 percent in 1956, 65 percent in 1968, and 60 percent in 1980. At the same time, the median percentages of time spent in research and writing activities were 3.6 percent in 1956, 10.4 percent in 1968, and 5.3 percent in 1980. Even at the flagship Minneapolis-St. Paul University of Minnesota campus the figures were 13 percent in 1956, 23 percent in 1968, and 20 percent in 1980. It was the case, however, that although attention to teaching had not greatly diminished over the years, the proportion of faculty reporting publications, presentations at professional meetings, and other types of creative work increased between 1968 and 1980. This was particularly true at the University of Minnesota.[7] All of this suggests that although faculty may have become more involved in research, they have not necessarily become less involved in teaching.

Yet, many faculty are convinced that a disregard for teaching is the bane of academic life, and they believe they know the source of the problem: too great an emphasis on research. Three of four faculty at four-year institutions believe that it is difficult to achieve tenure in their department if one does not publish.[8] (The number of faculty who believe this increased by nearly 50 percent in the last two decades.[9]) It is an article of faith, encountered time and again, that if one is busy doing research and publishing in order to hold a job, one must be ignoring teaching responsibilities and students. The dubious assumption here is that there is a constant resource pool that can be equally well employed engaged in teaching or in research. At four-year institutions, faculty are equally divided between agreeing and disagreeing that the pressure to publish is largely responsible for reducing the quality of teaching.[10]

The belief that research and publication are significantly more important than teaching for a successful academic career, and are becoming more so, is widely held—and is particularly dismaying to faculty who place the highest value on teaching. (All surveys find that faculty attach a great deal of importance to teaching.) Although over half are convinced that it is difficult to receive tenure if one does not publish,[11] nearly two-thirds of the professoriate believe that teaching effectiveness should be the primary criterion for promotion. Almost half of the faculty at four-year institutions agree that teaching effectiveness should be the primary criterion for promotion. Even in research universities, over 20 percent of the faculty believe this.[12] Although in the last twenty years at all types of institutions the proportion holding this view has steadily decreased from about eight in ten to six in ten, it is still a dominant belief, except in universities.[13]

A 1987 survey of almost 2,500 chairs of academic departments conducted by the United States Department of Education's National Center for Educational Statistics found that when hiring new faculty they considered a candidate's teaching quality, highest degree level, and program needs—in that order—the three most important factors. Three-fourths reported they considered teaching quality a key factor. However, at institutions that grant doctorates, chairs were more concerned about the quality of an applicant's research than about teaching; 45 percent considered the latter a very important factor, while 73 percent considered the former to be so.

In evaluating junior colleagues for tenure, almost 90 percent of the chairs agreed that teaching quality was very important. This was true for only two-thirds of the chairs in doctoral-granting institutions; 84 percent of these chairs rated quality of research and 77 percent rated quality of publications as very important.[14] In Burke's study of the hiring process at major research universities in the 1980s, it was found that "the emphasis on teaching...commitment to teaching, teaching experience, and a presentation that displays a potential for teaching were mentioned frequently" as selection criteria.[15]

According to the National Center for Educational Statistics, in 70 percent of the 31,000 academic departments in four-year institutions, quality of teaching is considered most important in hiring entry-level, full-time faculty. (Two other factors ranked higher: whether or not an individual had the appropriate highest degree, 80 percent, and programmatic needs, 71 percent.) In 84 percent of the departments, quality of teaching was considered very important in granting tenure. Not surprisingly, for both selection of faculty and tenure decisions, less emphasis was placed on teaching ability at doctoral granting institutions than at those that focused on undergraduate education. Student evaluations were used in rating the teaching performance of faculty in almost all departments.[16]

A comparison of policies and practices with regard to the evaluation of faculty in four-year liberal arts colleges in 1983 and 1993 clearly shows that in making decisions on retention, promotion, or tenure, classroom teaching—with remarkable consistency—was the "major factor" in assessing performance over the ten-year period. For both surveys, deans were given a list of thirteen criteria and were asked to rate each as major or minor. Classroom teaching ranked first at both points of time; in 1983, 98.7 percent of the 616 deans reported that it was a major factor, and in 1993, 98.7 percent of the 501 deans reported that it was a major factor. In both surveys, student advising ranked second, being mentioned as a major factor by about 60 percent of the deans.

The deans were also asked which of fifteen sources of information were used to evaluate teaching performance. Five of the fifteen (alumni opinions, follow-up studies of students, grade distribution, student examination performance, and enrollment in elective courses) were "always used" by fewer than 10 percent of the colleges in both periods. In 1983, evaluation by department chair (81.3 percent) was most commonly used, followed by evaluation by dean (75.0 percent) and systematic student ratings (67.5 percent). In 1993, systematic student ratings (85.7 percent) was most commonly used, followed by evaluation by department chair (78.7 percent) and evaluation by dean (67.9 percent). Five of the fifteen sources were used more often by at least 5 percent of the colleges in 1993 than in 1983, while only one (evaluation by dean) was used less often. These increases, most particularly in classroom visits (from 19.8 percent in 1983 to 33.4 percent in 1993), suggest that attempts to gather information became more systematic and structured over the ten-year period. [17]

On the other hand, research by the Stanford Project on Academic Governance indicates that undergraduate teaching is given less weight in the evaluation process than the percentage of time people spend on it, while "research is greatly overstressed" (that is, "is evaluated higher than is justified by the time spent on it").[18] This is consistent with Caplow and McGee's finding that faculty in research universities were primarily evaluated on the basis of their research. Indeed, according to Caplow and McGee, not only was teaching not rewarded at these institutions, but "academic success is likely to come to the man who has learned to neglect his assigned [teaching] duties in order to have more time and energy to pursue his private professional interests."[19]

Given the expressed general commitment by the American professoriate to teaching, some might expect it would be adequately rewarded, that there would be obvious returns, particularly for those who excelled in the classroom. However, if we look at extrinsic or tangible rewards—obtaining a position, salary level, merit salary increases, the awarding of tenure, rates of promotion, office and clerical support, course assignments, and other emoluments—or intrinsic or symbolic rewards—honors and esteem—there is little evidence that this occurs. Those who do the most or are said to be the best teachers are not the most highly rewarded. It would seem that the law of supply and demand is at play here.

The smaller rewards for efforts at teaching compared to efforts at research can in part be explained by two facts: more faculty prefer teaching to research, and there is a greater demand for those with the aptitude or ability to do research rather than teaching. Put plainly, there is a scarcity of researchers relative to teachers. If the supply of those with particular skills is great in relation to their demands, rewards do not have to be particularly high, and, in fact, increases in the supply of those able to perform a task will cause the general level of income to decline over time. Income is generally higher for an activity when the demand for it remains high or when there is more demand than supply of it.

And economists know there is more than supply and demand operating here. A teacher serves and nurtures students, and they have found that, *ceteris paribus*, individuals with a self-expressed taste for helping others do not earn as much than those less inclined to do so.[20]

It is because teaching is a negligible factor in the academic marketplace that it excludes most of the professoriate. The career prospects of those who teach are governed by internal submarkets, namely those colleges and universities where they happen to be located. The terms and conditions of their mobility and income are determined not by a national market, but by distinctive (local) institutional rules and procedures.

The Growth of Research and the Cost to Teaching

In recent years research has become more and more central to institutions of higher learning, while instruction of undergraduates has become less so. Since the late 1950s, there has been an increase in the availability of research funds, particularly in the early years from the federal government, for college and university faculty. As a consequence, the proportion contributed to the total income of many institutions of higher learning from student tuition and fees has decreased. Tuition and fees have become a smaller part of institutional budgets. As Geiger points out, at the extreme, since 1946 the MIT budget for organized research has dwarfed that for instruction: "In fact, these research funds supported far larger and more prestigious departments than instruction per se could ever have justified."[21] On average, for doctoral universities, income from tuition and fees provide for about one-sixth of total expenditures, while one-fifth of their direct support comes from the federal government.

During the 1960s, institutions of higher learning doubled their share of the nation's research and development expenditures from 5 to 10 percent, and this figure has remained fairly stable since then. In the decade 1958–68, research and development in institutions of higher learning grew by 371 percent; almost 80 percent of the increase came from the federal government.[22] [The national total for research and development in 1988 was $125 billion; academic research and development increased from $2 billion (in 1988 dollars) in 1958 to $13 billion in 1988.] [23] In 1989, colleges and universities spent an estimated $15 billion on research and development; about $9 billion of this came from the federal government. The research and development expenditures for college and universities increased twenty-five-fold between 1960 and 1990: 1960—$646 million; 1970—$2,335 million; 1980—$6,076 million; 1990—$16,624 million.

In recent decades the growth in the involvement in basic research of institutions of higher learning has also been significant. Their overall share of basic research expenditures grew from 25 percent in 1953 to 50 percent of the 1988 total of $18 billion.[24]

It is also worth noting that the federal government encouraged the growth of graduate programs—and hence, research—with direct subsidies to graduate students and the departments in which they enrolled through the National Defense Education Act of 1958. Further, in 1960, the Seaborg Commission (the President's Science Advisory Committee) recommended doubling the number of universities (from between fifteen to twenty to between thirty to forty)—thus, greatly increasing the number of faculty and graduate students—that would be deemed capable of conducting significant research. By 1968, forty-one universities were receiving more than $10 million a year from the federal government for research and development.

Universities have been significantly increasing the number of organized research centers. In 1980, there were 1507; in 1985, there were 2140—an average of forty-eight among the twenty-five leading research universities and twenty-three among the next seventy-five research universities. At the same time, the percent of federal research and development funds allocated to the ten leading research universities has declined markedly: it was 46 percent in 1954, 37 percent in 1958, 28 percent in 1968, 26 percent in 1975, and 22 percent in 1987.

From 1958 to 1988 the largest proportion of increases in operating revenues for institutions of higher learning came from state and local governments, and not tuition increases.[25] Tuition generated from undergraduates simply is not as necessary for the financial well being of many institutions of higher learning as in the past. This is true in spite of steeply rising tuition costs in recent years. Tuition and fees account for slightly less than 40 percent of the revenues of private institutions and between one-sixth and one-seventh of the revenues of public institutions. As incredible as it might seem, the total cost for tuition, fees, room and board of close to $25,000 and more at a number of the more expensive schools for the 1993-94 academic year only paid for about two-thirds of the cost of educating an undergraduate.

And it would not be an easy matter to increase tuition and fees—which in 1992-93 were on average $2,300 at four-year public institutions and $10,500 at four-year private institutions—in the short term to raise revenue for the teaching program. In public institutions they increased by nearly 110 percent, and in private institutions by 145 percent during the 1980s. This increase was much steeper than the rate of inflation, which was 64 percent, and wage and salary increases for most

Americans during this period. (Actually, on the average, real income declined by 6 percent.) In addition, the federal government's contribution for undergraduate scholarships decreased in the 1980s.

In fact, since the middle 1970s, the federal government's financial support for higher education has mostly slowed, and in some cases decreased. Federal fellowship support, which was at a high of $447 million in 1967, declined to $185 million by 1977. In 1968, the federal government was supplying almost one-third of the capital funds expended by universities; in the 1980s, the figure was one-eighth. According to the National Science Foundation, the share of separately-budgeted university research and development supported by federal funds was as follows:

Year	Percent
1953	53
1960	63
1966	74
1976	67
1987	63[26]

By the 1980s federal money—which had seduced many academic administrators and faculty, leading them to become disconnected from students in the 1960s and 1970s—was less plentiful, and there was considerable risk in continuing to expect federal largesse.

In short, before the days when institutions of higher learning began to receive large sums of research money from federal and state governments, foundations, and businesses, they were quite dependent on the tuition generated by undergraduates. It was fiscally prudent that they keep students satisfied—and enrolled. However, large research grants made them more independent, less dependent, and freed them of the tyranny of keeping their classrooms full. There are now other sources of funds, but these are finite; no one has the resources of the federal government.

Faculty who have been and are now involved in activities other than teaching, who are doing research and getting funds to do so, clearly contribute to keeping an institution's books balanced. Instruction may not even be a very important consideration in the hiring of some faculty. The trend since the 1960s toward lighter teaching loads, more generous faculty travel and leave programs, and providing campus research facilities may look like poor policy and planning—diverting funds that could best be put to instructional purposes—but it has given faculty a greater ability to engage in the cycle of completing research and applying for research grants in order to add to a school's reputation and coffers, particularly in light of the increasingly intense competition for each research dollar.

All of this is complicated by the fact that the federal government's contribution to academic research noticeably leveled off in the 1980s, leaving many institutions with massive research establishments to sustain. Given the increasingly intense competition for research funds, it has become necessary for many universities to expend more of their own funds on research and public relations in order to attract more external research support. The economic future looks bleak for those whose return have been about the same as their expenditures. At best, they seem to be running in place.

The Effects of College

The lack of extrinsic rewards for good or effective teaching seems particularly perplexing to those who hold that college attendance engenders a broad array of changes in students, many that go well beyond simple gains in verbal, quantitative, and subject matter competence. It is widely believed that as a result of their classroom experiences students, among other things, learn critical thinking, become more intellectually flexible, become more sensitive to principled moral issues, become less authoritarian, and develop morally. It has thus become an article of faith that teaching, the activity the early pages of this chapter have made clear most faculty spend the majority of their time doing, has added socially valuable and significant consequences; that from the work of faculty students gain cultural awareness which is the basis of good citizenship and learn the skills for questioning the status quo, which provides an impetus for effective change.

There have been hundreds of studies to determine the effects of the undergraduate years, and the mass of evidence indicates that attending college has only a modest and mostly ill-defined impact on students.[27] Quite simply, four years of college barely changes the vast majority of students: generally not a great deal of learning goes on in the classroom, and students leave college looking much as they did when they entered.

Given how little students change in college, it can and has been argued that it is not necessary to reward outstanding effort at or apparent success in teaching. Teaching is not a productive activity, and adds little to productivity. It is necessary to look at this argument with some care.

It would not be a gross distortion to assert that much of college teaching has a marginal social impact. To be sure, in the course of four years, undergraduates do learn something. Perhaps they do not learn as much as faculty believe they teach them, and admittedly not all of this is acquired in the classroom, but there is no denying they do learn something. This, however, may not be enough to settle the question of how much teaching matters; before a case can be made for the productivity of teaching, we need to know more about the effects of college on students. We need to know what students learn. And of what they learn, what of this do they get from faculty?

It cannot be denied that some learning occurs throughout the undergraduate years. Beginning as freshmen, students make some gains in factual knowledge (although research findings do not suggest that they generally become more knowledgeable because of what they major in) and in a range of cognitive and intellectual skills. In addition to acquiring knowledge of specific subjects and marginally developing cognitive skills such as critical thinking, there is evidence of modest gains in general verbal and quantitative skills. Yet, not much else happens. The net effects in oral communication skills, written communication skills, ability to use reason and evidence to address ill-structured problems, and intellectual flexibility are unclear. Moreover, the magnitude of change in general intellectual and analytical skill development is also unclear. All in all, the weight of the accumulated evidence is not terribly impressive.

Although it has been shown that something may sometimes be learned, if one looks at the total picture of what changes are possible but are seldom evident, one would have to conclude that in the broadest sense college makes a small difference. In the first place, whatever effects there are tend to persist in large measure as a result of living in a post-college environment that supports those effects. If individuals use what they learn, they retain some of it. If they do not use what they have learned, it is lost.

Of course, most would agree that there is more to the undergraduate experience than intellectual gains, the acquiring of information, and achievement. There is ideally the examination and development of attitudes and values, and there is psychosocial development. There is the expectation that the collegiate experience will broaden one's societal perspective and shape character. In all of these aspects students remain remarkably untouched by academic experiences. It would seem that college cannot change students, not merely that it does not change them.

Almost all studies make evident the illusory nature of psychological change on campus. Students are pretty well inoculated against all but superficial challenges. The magnitude of the effect of the collegiate experience on aesthetic, cultural, and intellectual values is unclear. The magnitude of the effect on the value placed on extrinsic occupational rewards is small, and unclear on intrinsic occupational rewards. The net effects of college on attitudes and values relating to social tolerance, political tolerance, civil rights and liberties, secularism, and modern gender roles are either unclear or small. Changes in identity and ego development are unknown. Changes in academic self-concept, social self-concept, self-esteem, and personal adjustment are small. Changes in autonomy, authoritarianism, dogmatism, ethnocentrism, interpersonal relations, maturity, and personal development are unclear. Research by psychologists and other behavioral scientists has not been able to show more.[28]

The most comprehensive longitudinal study—comparing individuals with different levels of educational attainment—to examine the long-term effects of higher education concluded that going to college barely touched values, life goals, or motivation for constructive social engagement: "Where higher education fails is in affecting seriously the expressive side of the lives of these alumni, their leisure activities and goals, their view of self, and to a lesser degree, their civic participation. There is precious little evidence that higher education really contributes to the personal development of its students beyond certifying them."[29] Socialization that did occur was as likely the result of experiences outside as inside the classroom.

Annual surveys of American college students done by the University of California at Los Angeles and the American Council on Education are the best reminders of the extraordinary stability in attitudes toward politics, life styles, and ideology of undergraduates. To be sure, during the 1960s students became more liberal, and their choice of majors reflected a concern with social activism and service. (It has often been shown that little of this came from faculty.) In the 1970s and 1980s students of the "me generation" flocked to fields such as law and business, fields that might yield high incomes.[30] However, students come to campus with these predispositions. Student generations change because young people are affected by the same societal trends and conditions as the rest of the population; change, at least not a great deal of change, does not happen while they are students.

Even the much-studied women from Bennington College, who were saturated with New Deal ideas and idealism in the 1930s, were not discernibly different when compared with their sisters and other close relatives in later years. Spouses and children, community activities, and social class were clearly more salient than vaguely remembered Keynesian and liberal ideas imbibed on campus.[31] The effects of education on students' personalities was not enduring.

To believe that the values and beliefs of faculty are transmitted to and uncritically adopted by students is simply part of a self-serving mythology. What someone might have heard (or read) as an undergraduate is unlikely to modify his or her behavior. The evidence is overwhelming: the impact on the American character or social structure of having thousands of students each year read Chaucer or Twain or struggle through freshmen calculus is inconsiderable. Values and character are formed in primary groups such as families and close friendships.

And in many courses students do not study Chaucer, Twain, or calculus. From the Rutgers catalogue for the 1993–94 academic year, undergraduates could instead choose "Hatha Raja Yoga," "California Aerobics," or "Hypnosis." At the University of Alaska, students could take "Introduction to Camping and Backpacking," or for the more skilled, "Advanced Backpacking." Students in the midwest who could not make it to Memphis could enroll in "American Popular Arts: Elvis as Anthology" at the University of Iowa. Some might hope that such offerings would have no lasting effects.

The case that the academic experience of the undergraduate years transforms students—and that, therefore, teaching faculty are productive—must rest on something more than that they learn and retain some of what they heard in the classroom. Again, this is not to deny that during college some students change. (Some do not change at all, and most who change do not change very much.) It is unclear, however, the degree to which any change can be attributed to academic experiences, the college experience in general, or something else completely extraneous to the collegiate experience. Change may be due to living in a dormitory, involvement in extracurricular activities, or normal maturation, and not necessarily due to contact with faculty or even with the curriculum or books.

Wilson found that only one-quarter of the personal changes reported by a sample of Antioch College students were attributed to courses and teachers. Of the 1,412 changes (intellectual, development of interest in new fields, worldview and personal philosophy, personality development, social development, career plans and choices, attitude toward the college) reported, 17 percent were attributed to the impact of a course and another 8 percent were attributed to teaching faculty. These two factors accounted for 37 percent of the changes in the intellectual sphere. Work experience, maturation, fellow students, education (experience) abroad, family members, the culture of Antioch, books and authors not related to a course, physicians or ministers or other significant adults accounted for most of the reported changes. This was in Wilson's words "a disenchanting estimate of academic power."[32]

In discussing what students get from any course, Wilson has observed:

> We do not know, usually, what the student's concurrent experiences may be contributing to the outcome: roommates and other peers, the mass media, the impact of other courses, and the like. And even if we could, with absolute certainty, attribute change to the beneficial impact of our course, we seldom know what elements of the course—books, lab work, fieldwork, homework, scintillating lectures—produced what effects, in what measure. It is at least conceivable that the professor, having orchestrated the experiences that make the course, could absent himself with no discernible diminution in changes effected in the student.[33]

The measure of a successful teacher is the ability to impart knowledge and promote intellectual activity in students. The quality of a teacher can only be determined by assessing that part of the achievement of students that results from teaching. Yet, research findings make it clear that the undergraduate experience barely changes the vast majority of students in a meaningful way, and that faculty do not make much of a difference in altering student ideologies or in broadening their societal perspectives. It is a conceit, clearly not something based on the weight of the evidence, to believe otherwise. It is certainly a mistake to assume, as do Bowen and Schuster, that "as educators [the nation's college and university faculties] directly influence the personal development and ideals of a large fraction of each successive generation."[34] Given the additional research finding that students do not learn the most from "effective teachers,"[35] it is perhaps not much of an overstatement to argue that to reward faculty for shining in the classroom is to give them credit for what happenstance, popular culture, and nature have done.

Again, consistent with economic theory, which holds that the greater the productivity of an activity the greater its demand and rewards, it could not be expected that, given how little undergraduates get from college, that teaching would be generously rewarded. Of course, in most cases teachers do not have to teach students much. It is only necessary that the institution certify to potential employers that a student has passed a prescribed number of courses to qualify for a degree. Employers want an individual with a college diploma for certain jobs, and will not hire someone without one. Someone with a degree has thus seemingly been made more productive, but when all is said and done it is the degree that places individuals in a position to be productive, not learning—not the work of teachers.

Individuals' capacities are not necessarily changed by education. The college or university experience is less important for what individuals are taught than for classifying and assigning them a social position. Higher education is a sorting device. A college degree is a credential that creates opportunities. It bestows social status whether students learn anything or not. When someone completes the required credit hours, he or she is identified as a college graduate. Those who fulfill the necessary requirements are marked as different, as somehow changed. Yet, in reality, a college education is more than anything else a credential, not an indicator that graduates have gained knowledge, that their teachers have been effective.

It would appear that those who only teach rarely discover, preserve, or communicate knowledge—all of which are at the core of higher learning.

Notes

1. Ernest L. Boyer, *Scholarship Reconsidered: Priorities of the Professoriate* (Princeton, N.J.: Carnegie Foundation for the Advancement of Teaching, 1990), 44.
2. Carolyn J. Mooney, "New U.S. Survey Assembles a Statistical Portrait of the American Professoriate," *Chronicle of Higher Education* (7 February 1990): A15 and A18.
3. Everett Carll Ladd, Jr., "The Work Experience of American College Professors: Some Data and an Argument," *Current Issues in Higher Education—1979* (Washington, D.C.: American Association for Higher Education, 1979): 9, table 6.

4. Elaine El-Khawas, *Campus Trends, 1992* [Higher Education Panel Report, (Washington, D.C.: American Council on Education, 1992)], table 12.
5. Everett Carll Ladd, Jr. and Seymour Martin Lipset, "Only 12 Percent of U.S. Faculty Members Think 'Intellectual' Describes Them Best," *Chronicle of Higher Education* (19 April 1976): 14.
6. Boyer, *Scholarship Reconsidered,* table A-26.
7. Reynold Willie and John E. Stecklein, "A Three-Decade Comparison of College Faculty Characteristics, Satisfactions, Activities, and Attitudes," *Research in Higher Education* 16 (March 1982): 81-93.
8. Boyer, *Scholarship Reconsidered,* table A-1.
9. Ibid., 12, table 1.
10. Ibid., table A-32.
11. Ibid., table A-1.
12. Ibid., table A-23.
13. Ibid., 29, 31, table 4.
14. "A Descriptive Report of Academic Departments in Higher Education Institutions," 1988 National Survey of Postsecondary Faculty (U.S. Department of Education, Office of Educational Research and Improvement, January 1990), section 3.
15. Dolores L. Burke, *A New Academic Marketplace* (Westport, Conn.: Greenwood Press, 1988), 65.
16. "A Descriptive Report of Academic Departments in Higher Education Institutions."
17. Peter Seldin, "How Colleges Evaluate Professors: 1988 vs. 1983," *AAHE Bulletin* 41 (March 1989): 3-7, and Peter Seldin, "How Colleges Evaluate Professors: 1983 v. 1993," *AAHE Bulletin* 46 (October 1993): 6-8, 12.
18. J. Victor Baldridge, et al., *Policy Making and Effective Leadership* (San Francisco: Jossey-Bass, 1978), 109.
19. Theodore Caplow and Reece J. McGee, *The Academic Marketplace* (New York: Basic Books, 1958), 221.
20. P. Taubman, *Sources of Inequality in Earnings* (Amsterdam and New York: North-Holland/Elsevier, 1975).
21. Roger L. Geiger, "Organized Research Units—Their Role in the Development of University Research," *Journal of Higher Education* 61 (January/February 1990): 12.
22. Ibid., 13.
23. *Science and Technology in the Academic Enterprise: Status, Trends, and Issues,* A Discussion Paper (Washington, D.C: National Academy Press, October 1989), 2-14 and 2-22.
24. Ibid., 2-18.
25. Ibid., 2-37.
26. Roger L. Geiger, "The American University and Research," in *The Academic Research Enterprise within the Industrialized Nations: Comparative Perspectives* (Washington, D.C.: National Academy Press, March 1990), 15-35.
27. Philip E. Jacob, *Changing Values in College: An Exploratory Study of the Impact of College Teaching* (New York: Harper & Row, 1957), and Kenneth A. Feldman and Theodore M. Newcomb, *The Impact of College on Students: An Analysis of Four Decades of Research* (San Francisco: Jossey-Bass, 1969).
28. Ernest T. Pascarella and Patrick T. Terenzini, *How College Affects Students* (San Francisco: Jossey-Bass, 1991), especially chapter 13.

29. William E. Knox, Paul Lindsay, and Mary N. Kolb, *Does College Make a Difference?: Long-Term Changes in Activities and Attitudes* (Westport, Conn.: Greenwood Press, 1993), 188.

30. Eric L. Dey, Alexander W. Astin, and William S. Korn, *The American Freshman: Twenty-Five Year Trends* (Los Angeles: Higher Education Research Institute, UCLA, 1991).

31. Theodore M. Newcomb, et al., *Persistence and Change: Bennington College and Its Students after 25 Years* (New York: John Wiley & Sons, 1967).

32. Everett K. Wilson, "The Entering Student: Attributes and Agents of Change," in Theodore M. Newcomb and Everett K. Wilson (eds.), *College Peer Groups: Problems and Prospects for Research* (Chicago: Aldine, 1966), 88–91.

33. Everett K. Wilson, "Apartheid and the Pathology of Sociology Instruction," in Frederick L. Campbell, Hubert M. Blalock, Jr. and Reece McGee (eds.), *Teaching Sociology: The Quest for Excellence* (Chicago: Nelson-Hall, 1985), 44.

34. Howard R. Bowen and Jack H. Schuster, *American Professors: A National Resource Imperiled* (New York: Oxford University Press, 1986), v.

35. Pascarella and Terenzini, *How College Affects Students,* 112.

4

Factors Affecting Rewards in Academia

In the last twenty five years there have been many attempts to determine what factors affect academic rewards, especially salary, and all show the same thing: the returns for teaching—good or bad, prodigious or desultory—are as a matter of course inconsequential. It seems reasonable to conclude that the distribution of valued items (in this case, academic salaries) reflects actual priorities and organizational exigencies.

Current research indicates that what individuals describe as effort or relative success with regard to teaching is for the most part unrelated to rewards, although there is some evidence that those who spend an inordinate amount of time teaching are actually disadvantaged in terms of salary. Faculty who spend the most time on research and publish more as a rule have higher salaries than their teaching-oriented colleagues. The nature of their work enables them to compete in the academic labor market. Holding type of four-year institution constant, bivariate analyses and cross-tabulations generally show negative relationships between various measures of teaching activity and salary and positive relationships between research activity and salary.[1]

Countless studies of organizational and career advancement for academics have found a number of factors related to salary level: highest earned degree, length of time to earn degree, quality or prestige of graduate institution, research productivity (primarily the publication of articles and books), ability to obtain research grants, institutional service, time spent on administrative work, public service, type of employing institution, geographic location of institution, discipline, years of experience or service, rank, gender, marital status, race, family background, and meritorious teaching. Taken together, the performance variables, including effort and success in teaching, account for a relatively small proportion of the salary differential among faculty. By itself, the rewards for teaching are at best marginal. (Hardly surprising, there is some evidence that teaching receives relatively more weight in those institutions that focus primarily on undergraduate education.) Generally the best predictor of salary within an institution and within any rank are an individual's years of experience. Just knowing how long someone has been around tells us more about his or her salary than having detailed information about the quality (or quantity) of scholarship or teaching.[2]

Katz found that even in a major public university, experience explained a sizable amount of variation in salary. His data also indicated notable differences in the salaries of males and those who had obtained graduate degrees from a prestigious department compared to females and those from a less highly ranked department. There were moderate rewards for those who succeeded in publishing articles and books, but not for those who succeeded in teaching.[3] In another study, Siegfried and White were able to show that within a single economics department, years of experience, the publication of articles, and having held an administrative position were related to salary, while students' evaluations of teaching were not. Having had administrative duties increased salary an average of $5209; outstanding teaching increased it by $732, not a statistically significant amount.[4]

Using material gathered from 301 colleges and universities by the American Council on Education, Tuckman found that the salaries of males who received an outstanding teaching award were on average $174 more than the salaries of those who did not receive one. This amount is about one-third of that received by those who engaged in unpaid public service, and only one-eighteenth of that received by those who held administrative positions. The salaries for females who received a teaching award were not even positively affected.[5] After additional detailed analysis of the data, Tuckman concluded: "Those with outstanding teaching awards seldom receive a salary increment in recognition of their skills; when they do, it tends to be considerably smaller than the increment received by those who publish. This finding holds true for all of the twenty-two fields analyzed."[6] Even at Macalester College, an institution known for dedication to the teaching and learning of undergraduates, nomination by students as an outstanding teacher was not found to be related to either rank or salary and nomination by faculty colleagues as an outstanding teacher was unrelated to rank and only modestly related to salary.[7]

The conclusion that background, merit, need, and attainment play an almost equal part in influencing academic salaries is not beyond what one would expect. Yet, it does contradict the widespread beliefs that there are significant rewards for academic performance, and that for the most part factors extraneous to academic performance do not affect salaries, or at most affect them only marginally. Given that ascription, achievement, and equity factors are all related to the distribution of rewards throughout society, these findings lend weight to the central point of chapter 2, namely, that colleges and universities are not that different from other institutions.[8]

Personal qualities may play some part in how effective teachers are in the classroom, but when this leads to rewards it is not usually because of this fact. For example, as every academic knows, being compatible or fitting in is a trait highly valued in the assessment of academics, and it is something that more often than not is rewarded. At the same time, compatibility is linked in the minds of many academics with the ability to teach. It is assumed that students are receptive to those whom they like. Given the line of argument in chapter 3 and to the degree that rewards are viewed as a function of productivity and of the market value of what is produced, it would not be expected that those whose compatibility presumably makes them effective teachers would be rewarded for this. But compatibility is rewarded, and this seems to be contrary to what economic theory would lead us to expect. Yet, it is not. All of the evidence suggests that compatibility can result in a higher salary if one is liked by colleagues. On the other hand, if students view someone favorably, it hardly matters. There can be material benefits if your colleagues find you "pleasant," "easygoing," or "a nice person." It barely makes any difference as far as salary goes what students think of you.

Besides classroom teaching, most faculty are also expected, in various degrees, to be involved in institutional service (i.e., committee assignments, administrative work, advising), public service (i.e., participation in professional organizations, consulting, government service), and research or scholarship. Thus, these other activities should also explain differential rewards. What is undeniably noteworthy, however, given what faculty do (most are primarily teachers) and say (that teaching is at the heart of the academic enterprise) and the pressure to reward putative teaching effectiveness, is that the measurable returns for teaching compared to those for other activities are so small.

It is well understood on campus that the rewards for teaching are meager. So many wring their hands about this state of affairs that obviously the reward system is not to the liking of many. Yet, the situation could hardly be different. There are a number of reasons teaching does not yield significant rewards, all dictated by the academic labor market. One need not be an economist to appreciate the cumulative effect when all of these factors are taken together.

Institutions and Disciplines

The academic marketplace, at least with reference to almost all four-year institutions, as one might conclude from the previous section, reflects the fact that a fully complete academic career is defined as involving both teaching and some research (in addition to sharing the responsibilities for the normal operation of the institution as an educational organization, that is, campus service and administration and some professional and community service). As a consequence, each academic has a career both in an organization and in a discipline. Besides being somewhere in the table of organization of a particular college or university, academics have identities within disciplines, and placement in the culture of a discipline is mostly a function of their putative contribution to the advancement of knowledge. Each of the parallel systems—the local system grounded in a college or university and the national or international (cosmopolitan) system grounded in a discipline—has its own prestige and reward hierarchy.

Teaching is an institutional activity and is identified only with the local prestige and reward hierarchies. It has limited visibility; it rarely brings national recognition and esteem; the reputation that comes from it is not easily portable. Research and publication transcend the campus; in large part their appraisal standards hold from institution to institution and even from country to country. While as a rule teaching is assessed internally, research and publication can be evaluated both internally and externally.

An individual's prestige is more often based on scholarly achievement than what he or she might have accomplished in the classroom (or even as an effective campus politician). Some of one's reputation in a discipline rubs off on his or her department; while little of one's reputation as a teacher does. Thus, one's scholarly reputation has value for other academics; one's teaching reputation does not. The scientific and scholarly accomplishments of researchers are signifiers of an institution's prestige.

To the degree that research is at least as highly valued as teaching, there are more opportunities for those who publish to convert prestige into monetary rewards. Professional visibility (read: having publications) can lead to overtures from other institutions. A college or university that would like to hold on to a faculty member who is being recruited elsewhere can offer a salary increase; a college or university that would like to hire a faculty member can bid for him or her. Quite obviously, the ability to move, portability, can have favorable economic outcomes. Put another way, those with the strongest record of publication have the most leverage to press for higher salaries. To be sure, those who publish may not often or successfully capitalize on their research accomplishments; however, it is never possible for those who only teach to do so. The chance to change academic positions is almost totally determined by disciplinary prestige, currency that teaching does not usually bring.

As we have been arguing, and as Caplow and McGee found,[9] the critical criteria in determining academic appointments are disciplinary prestige and, to a lesser extent, compatibility, which in the end make the operation of the academic labor market largely immaterial to most academics. In the evaluation of someone's teaching, personal qualities (e.g., one's reputation) are antecedent conditions; in contrast, as a scholar or scientist, the reverse is true. One's reputation as compatible contributes to one's putative contribution as a teacher. On the other hand, what one may have contributed to a discipline establishes one's reputation as a scholar or scientist. Moreover, someone who has published has produced intellectual property.

What one does as a scholar or scientist is relatively independent of one's life on a particular campus. One can attain professional prestige and success unimpeded by the hazards of the workplace or students. Campus friends and gossip are not completely unimportant, but they really do not matter when set against academic work well received by disciplinary colleagues, or a large research grant. The prestige of a researcher is independent of students, even for those who must rely on them for assistance in completing their work.

It is true that sometimes academic administrators do not acknowledge fully the research accomplishments of a faculty member, but generously reward someone whom they perceive as having given the institution extensive service, usually one of their own. Whether this does or does not happen, there is a strong possibility that disciplinary colleagues—that is, the larger scholarly community—will recognize research accomplishments through citations, research grants, and a range of awards, fellowships, lectureships, editorial appointments, honorary degrees and other honors, prizes, or board memberships or high office. These are symbols of visibility and esteem. The common rewards for an institutional career—rank, tenure, and salary—are more circumscribed. Those who put forth extraordinary efforts as teachers cannot generally expect a reduced teaching schedule, while those with funding for their research can purchase course release—and often a great deal more.

To be sure, institutions can and do provide time and support to facilitate disciplinary accomplishments. They do so at some price, as these accomplishments attach only ephemerally to institutions; they basically attach to individuals. They cannot be taken from individuals, but if individuals move elsewhere, they can be taken from institutions. Publishing books or articles enhances the prestige of both the scholar or scientist and the institution at which he or she holds an appointment. Individuals who have won recognition as scholars or scientists are worth a great deal to an institution, if only for purposes of public relations. If institutional authorities inadequately acknowledge someone's research accomplishments they are taking a risk, even more so if it is a seller's market, that the faculty member who may not feel fully appreciated will move elsewhere. An institution's administrators understands that if this should happen their efforts at self-promotion could be diminished.

Administrative Ambivalence

The capacity of colleges and universities and academic administrators to affect academic careers is minimized when in the evaluation of faculty research is placed above teaching. It should now be clear that the greater an individual's ties to the disciplinary prestige system, the weaker the hold of academic administrators. The greater the professional visibility, the greater the independence from administrative authority. (That is why the administrations of prestigious institutions are less autocratic than those of less esteemed institutions.)

For the most part, academic administrators do not have the ability to judge the quality of research. Some, those who have not been administrators for too many years, may be able to evaluate research in their own or in a cognate discipline. Yet, this is more effectively done by other specialists, often with appointments on other campuses. As Blau has observed,

> a faculty interested in research and capable of making research contributions has bargaining power that enables it to demand freedom from domination by centralized authority and to command greater influence in academic affairs as well as higher salaries. The academic accomplishments and prestige that enhance the faculty's power in relations with the administration depend, of course, not on formal qualifications alone.... Predominant concern with research also discourages administrative interference with appointment decisions for another reason. Research competence in an academic field evidently must be judged by experts in that field, whereas the same is not true for teaching competence, not merely because teaching skills are less highly specialized but particularly because academic faculties have no special expertness in teaching. Administrators' judgments about teaching may well be as good as physicists' or poets', but their judgments about physics or poetry surely are not. [10]

Academic administrators have created a dilemma for themselves. In promoting research, they have ceded some power and control to faculty. When researchers bring a campus notoriety and money, they also afford themselves some autonomy and, thus, it is hardly surprising that academic administrators have to some degree been reluctant to acknowledge that research is an essential part of the faculty's responsibilities.

Since in the decades after the Civil War, when the American professoriate began to pursue research as something more than a hobby or sideline, many academic administrators have tried to hold it in check. At the turn of the century, the official position at the University of Minnesota was that someone's research was "his own private business, much like playing the piano or collecting etchings."[11] The contention has been that teaching is a more noble, useful, and altruistic pursuit than research. The researcher is mostly interested in self-aggrandizement; the teacher is dedicated and self-sacrificing. Students are always victims.

The campaign has been unremitting. In 1870, Yale's Noah Porter sternly reminded faculty: "If a man desires to be a professor in an American college...he ought to have just conceptions of the nature of the work he desires. His official business is to educate the young, i.e., it is to teach and to train. This is the work for which the college exists, and the carrying forward which all its instructors, the professors included, are appointed.... The American college is not designed primarily to promote the cause of science by endowing posts in which men of learning and science may prosecute their researches, but to secure successful instruction for our youth.... [B]ut its aims should be primarily and distinctly directed to effective instruction as the chief end of its existence."[12]

Even after the turn of the century, there was no perceptible change in administrative priorities. In 1906 Stanford's president David Starr Jordan asserted: "The American university is emphatically a teaching university." More than three decades later at the University of Chicago, where research had first become an obsession, President Robert Maynard Hutchins publicly complained about "neglected" undergraduates.

Most recently, the refrain has been reiterated by Stanford's president Donald Kennedy—prior to his precipitous resignation in the wake of allegations that the university had misspent millions of dollars of government money intended to cover the overhead for research for expensive floral arrangements, custom-made bedding, antique furniture, and other nonacademic reasons: "There is a suspicion that we have lost focus in designing and delivering a well-planned, challenging and inspiring education to our undergraduates.... (Many of our best teachers of undergraduates) are undercompensated and unappreciated.... It is time for us to reaffirm that education—that is, teaching in all its forms—is the primary task, and that our society will judge us in the long run on how well we do it."[13] The resolute crusade has recruited countless present and former administrators, most notably Ernest Boyer and Page Smith.

The argument never changes: researchers are self-promoting egoists; those who teach keep the campus vital. Teaching is morally superior to research. In part due to these incessant allegations, in the minds of many, research implies a flight from teaching and a deficiency in institutional loyalty. Ordinary—that is, not ground-breaking—research and publication are belittled, as if they reflected greater incompetence than no research and publication at all. Only the most irresponsible teachers and teaching are demonized in this manner. Indeed, teaching is often seen as an all-or-nothing quality: one is expected to meet certain minimum standards, and after that one's ability in the classroom hardly matters. The rare public or formal complaints about teachers are more often about what students see as unreasonable standards than about the failure to demonstrate mastery of a subject. Grousing by students is often an echo first heard from the associate vice president for teaching effectiveness. Whatever other interpretation the denigration of research is given, it is not only an assault on faculty independence, it is an assault on quality; it benefits mediocrity in the name of a commitment to students and teaching.

It has become an article of faith that there is a basic conflict between research and teaching—that to do one well precludes doing the other well. While teaching is its own art and the best biology teacher is not necessarily the best biologist, the fact is that there is a great deal of evidence that teaching clearly profits from research. A convincing case has yet to be made that teaching is enhanced by deemphasizing research.

Because most academics publish nothing or very little (even at universities one-fifth of the faculty report that they have had "no professional writings accepted for publication in the last two years;" the figure for faculty at two-year colleges is four-fifths), the widespread idea that there is an inverse relationship between good teaching and good research leads to the conclusion that more faculty are good teachers than is the case. The assumption here is that if someone is not publishing, he or she must be a conscientious teacher. Indeed, it is commonly believed that most faculty are above-average teachers. (Here academia is not unlike Lake Woebegon, where all of the children are said to be above average.)

Success in research clearly affects organizational advancement. When colleges and universities recognize and reward those involved in research, they increase the likelihood of retaining faculty who can bring them grant money, recognition, and prestige. The prominence and research grants of faculty stars are invaluable. Faculty with visibility beyond the campus have a utility. They serve the same purpose as a successful athletic program. The quality of research cannot always be exactly determined, but there are rough indications of where someone stands in the professional pecking order. The disciplinary prestige of individuals redounds to their departments and institutions. The reputation of faculty in their disciplines has value to the institutions that employ them. As Gross and Grambsch put it, "prestige...conveys ideas of leadership, of power, and, above all, of excellence."[14] In the academic world, prestige is equated with quality. However, since teaching does not bring prestige, those who only teach are more often than not seen as having little or no academic quality. This bitter fact cannot be changed by demeaning those who chose to do research.

At the same time, as a criterion for disciplinary or institutional advancement, teaching does not have much exchange value. Good teaching is not known to bring more students and greater endowments. Achievements in teaching can be said to lack universal currency. Successful teaching generally does not make a contribution to a discipline. Successful teachers only occasionally (over a period of time) and mostly invisibly add to the betterment of the institution. Campus colleagues may have some inkling that there is an important historian among them. Disciplinary colleagues know about his or her books on the Civil War, but have no concern about what or if he or she teaches. Who is doing high-quality mathematics may be of interest to many in the discipline (and perhaps to some in cognate disciplines); who is doing high-quality teaching (often not easy to define) will get considerably less attention.

The campus reputation of faculty is of little consequence in the culture of a discipline. It does not advance a field in a way that the professional reputation of an individual may advance a college or university. Those who excel as researchers may be given or find other employment opportunities; knowledge of someone excelling in the classroom is seldom broadcast beyond the campus. Indeed, it has been shown that "the majority of faculty who see themselves primarily as teachers...do not have strong internal or external social ties in any work role area."[15] Teaching is clearly not something that is conducive to developing professional associations. Because faculty seldom visit each other in the classroom and know of each other's teaching mostly from hearsay, it is not likely to further relationships with colleagues.

One additional matter merits attention here. Research has shown that individuals learn about job openings more often through personal contacts than by other methods.[16] Those with fewer contacts will hear about fewer jobs, and as a consequence will be less active in the labor market. The more one participates in the labor market, the more likely one will find a job, which might be used to generate a counteroffer and salary increase from a local administrator. Obviously, those least involved in the labor market—those with only a local reputation—seldom have a chance to bargain about and increase their salaries.

Virtually the only option a faculty member who feels that his or her teaching commitment (or contribution) is not being adequately recognized by institutional authorities has is to reduce that commitment or wait and hope that there will be a banquet or testimonial expressing gratitude for extraordinary efforts in the classroom. The allocation of salaries or the entire reward structure within an institution is in part shaped by the disciplinary market situation. At the same time, disciplinary rewards are hardly affected by the intrainstitutional reward structure.

Those who espouse the functional theory of unequal rewards would add another reason why it is likely that teaching and research would be rewarded in a differential manner; the latter requires rarer skills, and those with the rarest skills are able to command greater compensation.

As the functionalists see it, teaching is an additive activity in that even when effectively done it does not affect the performance of others in an organization. Moreover, individuals engaged in teaching are seen as mostly interchangeable, more interchangeable than members of a baseball team or academics who engage in research. All teaching and teachers make a nearly equal contribution, and it makes little difference who does what. Individuals' contributions to a product are not only nearly equal but they are alike, as would be the case with assembly line workers or members of a symphony orchestra. On the other hand, there are relatively greater differences in the contributions of researchers. The differences in the capacities of effective teachers and less effective teachers are smaller than the differences in the capacities of effective and less effective researchers. Successful teaching may sometimes make other positions more productive, but successful research, because it is complementary, can often be depended on to make other positions much more productive. (This would also be the case with professional athletes, such as baseball pitchers, or stars of a play or movie.) There is some empirical support for this argument.[17]

Lotka's inverse-square law of productivity—that the number of researchers producing n papers is proportional to $1/n^2$—which has been confirmed several times, would lead one to conclude that few academic publish in a continuing or sustained manner because most are not capable of doing so. According to Lotka's calculations, 165 individuals will produce more than 586 papers in a lifetime, but only ten will write more than 50 percent of this total, and two will write 25 percent. The remaining 75 percent of the scientists write the other 25 percent. Looking at this another way, this means that for every 100 authors who write but a single paper, twenty-five write two, eleven write three, six write four, four write five, three write six, two write seven, two write eight, one writes nine, and so on. Indeed, the ability to make a scholarly contribution seems to be a rare skill.[18]

The demands of expanding knowledge created by industrial and post-industrial societies has placed less value on the generalist and more on the specialist. All academic disciplines have become more elaborated. Where there was once chemists, there are now organic, inorganic, analytical, and physical chemists. In research departments, there are bioinorganic and theoretical organic chemists. Those who choose greater specialization, who work to expand knowledge, must do more than teach and what they do is seen as more valuable than simply teaching.

Finally, the likelihood of complete failure in a research project appears to be greater than complete failure in a classroom. Research is a riskier enterprise than teaching. Teachers whose students learn little or nothing can still be liked by them; they may not feel that it has all been for naught. The feedback for teaching, at least compared to research, is immediate, personal and powerful. Favorable comments by students can make one feel successful and energized. It is easy for teachers to see themselves as competent and to feel satisfied; research projects take months or years to complete and their results are not always easy to publish. Researchers may need more to motivate them than do teachers.

Research is more often than not tedious, hard work. It brings researchers on campus in the evening and on weekends and holidays, while teaching seldom does. Writing up one's results can be torturous. Finding someone to publish a piece of research can be time consuming and troublesome. A publication in a prominent journal or with a recognized press is an accomplishment even for the most prolific and visible in their discipline. Scholarly publication is thus a special achievement. To the degree that Adam Smith's observation that the disadvantages of a pursuit restricts the supply of labor to demand and elevates rewards is correct, we would expect researchers to be scarcer, more valued, and more highly rewarded than teachers.

It is worth adding that few academics other than untenured faculty at research institutions are under much pressure to publish. Not many of the professoriate perish from failure to publish, and, as we will now see, time spent on research is in large part voluntary. At the same time, failure to meet minimal teaching obligations can result in sanctions, even the ultimate sanction of loss of tenure and dismissal. Academics must teach, but, with few exceptions, need not do research.

The Work Week

How many hours an individual works is not a perfect measure of productivity or contribution, but surely it is a fairly good way to calculate effort. It thus seems appropriate to look briefly at the amount of time faculty with a teaching orientation spend carrying out their academic responsibilities and contrast this to the amount of time those with a research orientation—who might be less involved with students, but more involved in a wider range of other activities—spend. The comparison below of the average length of the work week of faculty who are most committed to research with those who are less so, makes it quite clear that they work longer hours. This, by itself, can have obvious implications for relative rewards.

The data considered are from a single study: a recent survey of about 3500 American academics completed in 1991–92 by the Carnegie Foundation for the Advancement of Teaching. The respondents were asked to self-report how many hours a week they spent on teaching (preparation, classroom instruction, advising students, reading and evaluating student work), research (reading literature, writing, conducting experiments, fieldwork), service (to clients and/or patients, paid or unpaid consulting, public or volunteer service), administration (committees, meetings, paperwork), and other academic activities (attending conferences, other professional activities) when classes were in session and when they were not in session. The findings are unambiguous.

First, faculty whose interests lie primarily in teaching or in both teaching and research but lean toward teaching work a shorter work week, particularly when school is not in session, than those whose interests lie primarily in research or in teaching and research but lean toward research. Fewer than half of the former, while over two-thirds of the latter work forty-one hours a week or more when school is not in session.

Second, the relationship between number of articles published and length of the work week is positive and linear: the more articles an individual has published, the more hours he or she works each week whether or not school is in session. During the time when classes are scheduled, slightly more than one-third with no published articles work forty-one hours per week or more, while over 80 percent with seven or more published articles work that much. When classes are not in session, the differences are even greater: 34.1 percent of those who have published no articles work forty-one hours a week or more; 82.3 percent—over twice the number—of those who have published seven or more article work forty-one hours a week or more.

Third, those who teach only undergraduate students are less likely than those who teach both undergraduate and graduate students or teach only graduate students to work more than forty hours a week. This is particularly true when classes are not in session. When they have no immediate instructional responsibilities, almost two-thirds of those who teach only graduate students work more than forty hours a week; this figure is almost twice of that for those who teach only undergraduates.

Finally, when school is in session, there is little difference in the length of the work week between those with a heavy commitment to group instruction and those with lighter formal teaching loads. However, when school is not in session, about 50 percent more of the latter than the former work more than forty hours a week.

Taken together, these findings may point to yet another reason why those who are not involved in research are rewarded more modestly than those who are: overall, they do not seem to work as long, and possibly as hard.

Notes

1. James S. Fairweather, "Academic Values and Faculty Rewards," *Review of Higher Education* 17 (Fall 1993): 43–68.
2. Lionel S. Lewis, Richard A. Wanner, and David I. Gregorio, "Performance and Salary Attainment in Academia," *American Sociologist* 14 (August 1979): 157–69, and Martin J. Finkelstein, *The American Academic Profession* (Columbus: Ohio State University Press, 1984), 58–61.
3. David A. Katz, "Faculty Salaries, Promotions, and Productivity at a Large University," *American Economic Review* 63 (June 1973): 469–77, especially table 1.
4. John J. Siegfried and Kenneth J. White, "Financial Rewards to Research and Teaching: A Case Study of Academic Economists," *American Economic Review* 63 (May 1973): 313, table 1.
5. Howard P. Tuckman, *Publication, Teaching, and the Academic Reward Structure* (Lexington, Mass.: Lexington Books, 1976), 57.
6. Ibid., 76.
7. Jack E. Rossman, "Teaching, Publication, and Rewards at a Liberal Arts College," *Improving College and University Teaching* 24 (Autumn 1976): 239.
8. David I. Gregorio, Lionel S. Lewis, and Richard A. Wanner, "Assessing Merit and Need: Distributive Justice and Salary Attainment in Academia," *Social Science Quarterly* 63 (September 1982): 492–505.
9. Caplow and McGee, *The Academic Marketplace.*
10. Peter M. Blau, *The Organization of Academic Work* (New York: John Wiley & Sons, 1973), 169.

11. W. H. Cowley, "Three Curricular Conflicts," *Liberal Education* 46 (December 1960): 473.
12. Noah Porter, *The American Colleges and the American Public* [New York: Arno Press, 1969 (originally published in 1870)], 129-30.
13. Quoted in Don Wycliff, "Concern Grows on Campuses at Teaching's Loss of Status," *New York Times* (4 September 1990): A1 and B8.
14. Edward Gross and Paul V. Grambsch, *Changes in University Organization, 1964-1971* (New York: McGraw-Hill, 1974), 100.
15. Paul J. Baker and Mary Zey-Ferrell, "Local and Cosmopolitan Orientations of Faculty: Implications for Teaching," *Teaching Sociology* 12 (October 1984): 97. Moreover, Granovetter found that jobs offering the highest salaries are more likely to be found through personal contacts than through formal means or direct application. Since those who teach have fewer personal contacts than those who teach and do research, they would be less likely to find positions which would increase their earnings. [Mark S. Granovetter, *Getting a Job: A Study of Contacts and Careers* (Cambridge, Mass.: Harvard University Press, 1974), 15.]
16. Mark S. Granovetter, "The Strength of Weak Ties," *American Journal of Sociology* 78 (May 1973): 1371.
17. Mark Abrahamson, "Talent Complementarity and Organizational Stratification," *Administrative Science Quarterly* 18 (June 1973): 186-93. The point has already been made that researchers publish more, become more professionally visible, and as a consequence are more actively recruited by other institutions. Thus, their greater rewards might be due more to marketplace pressures than functionalists acknowledge.
18. Derek J. de Solla Price, *Little Science, Big Science...and Beyond* (New York: Columbia University Press, 1986), 38-42. See also Herbert A. Simon, *Models of Men: Social and Rational* (New York: John Wiley & Sons, 1967), chapter 9, especially p. 160. Alfred J. Lotka's analysis first using the decennial index of Chemical Abstracts for 1907-1916, "The Frequency Distribution of Scientific Productivity," was published in the *Journal of the Washington Academy of Sciences* 16 (19 June 1926): 317-23.

5

The Evaluation of Teaching and Research

There is an additional problem with respect to rewarding teaching in a way that might seem fair. In most occupations, an individual's work can be evaluated. This is not the case for the academic profession. Although most academic work is teaching, it is not easy to evaluate its quality. The products of teaching are difficult to measure, and success is difficult to quantify. As a consequence, its outputs cannot be well defined. If teaching cannot be effectively evaluated, it cannot be effectively rewarded. (Indeed, since students learn very little, it might in any case be an empty exercise to attempt to assess teaching effectiveness.)

Assessing Teaching Effectiveness

There is general consensus that teachers should have some knowledge to impart and some skill in imparting it, but the assessment of teaching involves a good deal more than simply ascertaining the knowledge and skills of a teacher, how material is presented, and even what has been learned by students. We do not know what the objective criteria should be for evaluating teaching, let alone how quality might be measured. Indeed, the question of assessing teaching effectiveness is such a tangled skein that the more it is held up to examination, the more it would appear that those who would have us ignore what goes on between faculty and students possess a sort of primeval wisdom.

First of all, it is evident that those who have attempted to measure teaching effectiveness have not sorted out the concept's various connotations. Some have simply equated effective teaching with good teaching. This, however, may be too simple, as one can inspire student to learn much trivia well. Moreover, there is not a great deal of consensus on what is meant by the term *good teacher*: someone with an outgoing and pleasant personality; someone who is popular and well-received; someone who is knowledgeable; someone who motivates good students; or someone who motivates marginal students. And, for that matter, what is meant by *outgoing, pleasant, popular, well-received, good* and *marginal,* and *motivates*?

There are many such questions, and few have been answered. As has been pointed out many times, this matter of explicitness is both complex and simple.

Why is a definition of good teaching so elusive? In one sense it is not elusive at all. You can define good teaching any way you like. Simply take any outcome, process, or quality that seems desirable, and then define good teaching as whatever something called a teacher does to bring it about efficiently. Even a cursory fishing in the literature will net such definitions by the dozen. Good teaching is what the "teacher" does to produce inspired pupils, excited pupils, interested pupils, creative pupils; pupils who are good citizens, who can read, do arithmetic problems and write grammatical English essays. Among other desiderata used to define good teaching are critical thinking, subject matter mastery, ideals, love of freedom, respect for law and order, universal brotherhood, various attributes of character, a love of learning and a devotion to the arts. I am sure one can add another hatful of items to this list.[1]

But again, what do *inspired, excited, interested, creative,* and the like mean? Even if we knew or could get agreement, "such definitions...tell us nothing about the factors which produce these results." It would seem that as thinking about the matter becomes more involved and convoluted, the notion of teaching effectiveness floats further from our grasp, becoming less specific and verifiable, more ecclesiastical than scientific. There are many, many questions, and whether an instructor is clear or approachable or challenges or gives appropriate information about progress or has fair and rigorous performance standards has not yet even been considered. There are too many kinds of good teaching to draw conclusions readily about relative quality.

Because teaching effectiveness is not easily or precisely conceptualized or defined, it is not easily measured. To start, we would have to know with what traits students enter a course, with what traits they leave, and what influences account for the differences, if any. If we measure what is transmitted, can we guess what is received? When do we measure what has been received?: at the end of a class period? at the end of the course? three months later? a year, five years, or ten years after graduation? And what is the most valid measure of effectiveness: what is communicated? what is understood? how a student is changed? In brief, "though they are worth seeking, precise before and after measures of teaching effectiveness are hard to envision."[2] The quality of any material which could be collected would be unreliable and of questionable validity. Because of the many variables, their many definitions, and the many ways they relate, it is accordingly difficult to assess teaching effectiveness—and the teaching role.

Undergraduate education is supposed to involve more than cognitive learning, that is, the acquisition of verbal skills, quantitative skills, substantive knowledge, rationality, and intellectual tolerance. Students are expected to develop emotionally and morally. They should learn something about themselves and others. As their human understanding increases and as they grow, so should their values. In some of their classwork they will also acquire competence in practical affairs—to become productive adults, effective family members, better citizens. How is all of this assessed?

It may be that giving any attention to what is transmitted in assessing teaching effectiveness is a waste of time. To know what is transmitted is not to know what is received. It might be best to concentrate on learning and more or less ignore teaching. Yet, this will not help in determining the quality of teaching, as very little is known—except at the extremes—about the relationship between teaching performance and student learning. The measures commonly used to judge either are not accurate. If the outputs of teaching are so indeterminate, how can its quality be evaluated so that it can be appropriately rewarded?

One final matter is worth considering. A large number of colleges and universities determine teaching quality using machine-scored student surveys. The top rated 10 to 15 percent are judged to be excellent teachers, and the bottom rated 10 to 15 percent are judged to be poor teachers. Those in between, the vast majority, are viewed as satisfactory. Moreover, it has long been known that the results of student evaluations of teaching are as closely related to factors, such as class size and the difficulty of the material, that have nothing to do with teaching or learning as with the competence of an instructor. In sum, the most commonly used procedure for evaluating instruction trivializes the assessment of teaching and teachers, and makes what goes on in the classroom appear to be of little consequence.

Assessing Research

It is considerably easier to assess research outputs. They are tangible. They are prized by other professionals (other experts), not lay persons, that is, students, many of whom are adolescents. Through publication, researchers establish mastery of a subject. In large part peers decide whether something is worth publishing in the first place. They referee and review articles and books. They may use them in their own work. Scholars and scientists perform for an audience of equals. Through publication, advances in knowledge come to be certified by members of a discipline.

Research does something for one's peers; teaching does not. And there are more standards for acceptable performance for research and publication. There are few, if any, explicitly stated standards for teaching. On the contrary, it is widely assumed that the long, grueling period of graduate training makes everyone competent in the classroom. (No one expects undergraduates to be discriminating consumers.) There are sometimes unasked and unanswered questions about highly rated teachers: Are they only amusing performers or entertainers? Have they merely repackaged readily available information?[3]

Since most academics are thought to be at least adequate teachers, the supply seems limitless. At the same time, it would appear from obvious variations in rates of publications that there are great differences in the scholarly ability of academics and a finite number of capable researchers. Because of all these factors, less of a premium is assigned to teaching. It is not necessarily that teaching is so complex that it is impossible to determine the relative competence of faculty with different styles; it is just that it is easier to evaluate other activities of faculty.

If all else fails, if the quality of the work of a scholar or scientist cannot be determined—if one believes that the reputation of a periodical in which an article was published, the reviews of a book, or the citations accorded a work are invalid measures of quality—the quantity can. Since more studies have than have not shown a positive relationship between the quality and quantity of academic work, this is not such a outrageous idea. (One commonly cited study of physicists found the relationship between quantity of publication and quality of publication to be .72.[4])

In his detailed study of the labor market experiences of 103 faculty members hired by fifty departments in eighteen large Southeastern institutions, Brown found that the hirer's knowledge of pertinent facts and opinions of job candidates was "grossly incomplete and imperfect."[5] Only five of the fifty chairs felt they knew all that they should have known about the qualifications of the person they hired. They acknowledged not knowing about such things as teaching ability, ability to work independently, reactions to particular teaching situations and environments, temperament and personality, and even physical appearance.

> In one instance a foreign-born man who had difficulty speaking English was hired without the hirer knowing about the difficulty. Another chairman mentioned an appointment he had made without knowing about two of the appointee's previous jobs and without knowing about the appointee's past record of major maladjustments. Other department chairmen had made appointments without knowing about the appointees' consuming interest in race relations, impending divorce, physical handicap, distance away from the Ph.D. degree, and forced move from previous job.[6]

Brown believes that this happens because the additional information obtained would not have been valuable enough to justify what it would have taken to collect it. In other words, marginal costs would have exceeded marginal benefits. The point is that in spite of the complex process of faculty recruitment and zealous efforts to collect what are believed to be facts about job applicants, departments may not know a great deal about those whom they hire.

Whatever the case, counting pages, articles or books seems to make some sense. (Since this can be done so quickly, one might even find time to read and evaluate some of the work.) Judging the scholarship of academics is difficult, and the length of someone's bibliography provides only a rough measure of ability. There is no such easy method for assessing teaching. Some academics insist that counting publications is not only crass but too imprecise to be meaningful. Yet, it is better at times to take the shadow for the substance than to disregard work that has undergone some editorial review, no matter how flawed the review— or the work.

The evaluation of teaching is essentially subjective as its quality is determined by the judgment of students, administrators, or peers. On the other hand, by counting articles and books, research can be objectively, although crudely, measured. (One could go even beyond totaling pages and use citation counts.[7]) It is the case, then, that the evaluation of teaching is not only more subjective, but also more ambiguous as outcome measures of research productivity are readily available. Those who spend their time doing research rather than teaching appear to be more competent and more deserving of greater rewards since generally objective qualifications outweigh subjective qualifications.

Research and Its Products as a Form of Teaching

A few more words about research seem in order. It is obvious that creativity is the foundation stone of excellence in American colleges and universities. Research and publication are symbolic of the creation of knowledge; teaching generally only involves the transmission of knowledge. Creation is a more visible and valued activity than transmission. The manifestation of innovative work may be traditional scholarly research, poetry, literary criticism, or the like.

It is not necessary that academics publish through established journals or even present their work in established ways; the research monograph has its place, but so does the essay-review, the synthesis of a field of study, or for that matter the well-argued polemic. Even microfiche, self-publishing, or the distribution of material in mimeographed form can play some part in the exchange of ideas. Whatever the work, it should be something that one's colleagues can evaluate. In the words of a former president of the American Association of University Professors, "publication is practically the only means by which the professor is brought to the judgment of his peers.... The test of presentation outside the college or university spurs accuracy, insight, and growth."[8]

The point has been made that teaching, which is also an integral part of the academic enterprise, is difficult to evaluate credibly—reliably, validly, and with consensus. At best, teaching evaluation can differentiate the most competent from the very worst classroom teachers. However, for the approximately 80 percent who fall in between these extremes, something more is needed. In institutions where the claim is made that faculties are engaged in a creative intellectual activity, teaching is simply not enough. The apologia that ideas can just as well be transmitted through the more informal means of a lecture, in a salon, or in a bull session as through a crafted manuscript is pure cant. Intellectual work is not a desultory activity, but demands careful exposition and examination that is generally not possible through verbal communication.

Productive scholarship is not only an essential side of the academic role, but also a necessary activity if one is to be an effective teacher.

Simply put, a teacher cannot remain stimulating unless he or she continues to learn. To be sure, teaching and research can and should reciprocally inform each other, but research certainly has more effect on teaching than the other way around. The research process involved in publication is without question the most potent form of learning. It demands not only disciplined reading and thinking, but the reporting of results which will be subject to review and criticism; it requires a precision in thinking not expected in a classroom situation. The printed page imposes a responsibility for care in thought not expected in speech; or, as Francis Bacon aptly put it: "Reading maketh a full man, conference a ready man, and writing an exact man."[9] A college or university instructor cannot do less than what he or she requires of students: to think incisively and organize and present written ideas effectively.

Furthermore, since at least the 1950s knowledge in most academic disciplines has been rapidly and continually changing at the hands of the prolific minority. Since producing publishable research requires keeping abreast of the latest developments in one's area, research almost guarantees that by keeping up-to-date with the advances in a discipline one will continue to learn—and be a more "effective" teacher.

Only some classroom instruction necessitates inventiveness or creative thought on the part of the professoriate. Some simply involves defining basic terms and ideas. Some involves exercise or drill. Some involves paraphrasing or amplifying the text. Lecture materials to supplement reading assignments can also be borrowed and distilled from other texts. The professor need not prepare an original lecture each time he or she steps into the classroom.

Publication is a form of teaching in that students and other teachers learn through reading. Someone who publishes has a far wider and potentially larger audience than someone who only conveys ideas in a classroom. As Samuel Johnson quipped: "Now, I cannot see that lectures can do so much good as reading the books from which the lectures are taken. I know nothing that can be best taught by lectures, except where experiments are to be shown."[10] Simply put, students do not have to be told things in order to learn them. A credentialed teacher is not required for learning to occur. To the degree that what is thought or written has any lasting value, it has more permanence in a library than in someone's memory. Even Noah Porter had to admit: "A remembered lecture is vastly inferior to a thoroughly mastered book, because the book will ordinarily be more condensed and scientific than the lecture, or, if not, more of it will be retained and placed methodically at the service of the learner."[11] Again, in sum, publication may help teaching; the reverse is almost never true.

If a person has nothing to publish, it may be that he or she has less of value to say to students than someone who has something to publish. In arguing that teaching and research are not "antagonistic," Jencks and Riesman found that "teachers cannot remain stimulating unless they also continue to learn," and this learning "is research by any reasonable definition. When a teacher stops doing it, he. begins to repeat himself and eventually loses touch with both the young and the world around him.... Publication is the only way a man [or woman] can communicate with a significant number of colleagues or other adults. Those who do not publish usually feel they have not learned anything worth communicating to adults. This means they have not learned much worth communicating to the young either."[12]

It would seem, then, that those who best fulfill the academic role, as most broadly defined, are most highly rewarded, which would scarcely classify as an electrifying conclusion.

For a number of years, the contention that good teaching shapes research, that new knowledge is readily acquired not only through the latter, but also through the former, has been pressed upon the academic community.[13] The intention here is to broaden the meaning of scholarship. The argument has been seen by some as a logical extension of two threads of post-modernist thought: that off-the-cuff ruminations—no matter how half-baked—put forward in a classroom by either faculty or students are as valid or valuable as those resulting from systematic research, and that professional associations and their publications are little more than hegemonic gatekeepers designed to prevent the distribution of ideas of the underclass by insisting on standards of objectivity. In any case, most university faculty have rejected this notion that teaching can be a substitute for published research on the grounds that it, in fact, seldom creates new knowledge.

Notes

1. H. S. Broudy, "Can We Define Good Teaching?" *The Record—Teachers College* 70 (April 1969): 583–84.

2. Kenneth E. Eble, "What Are We Afraid Of?" *College English* 35 (January 1974): 453.
3. Three researchers report conducting a study in which they used an actor to impersonate a lecturer who was reputed to be an authority on the application of mathematics to human behavior. The actor, who was well coached and looked distinguished, but who was completely ignorant of the topic, was instructed to teach "charismatically and nonsubstantively." The three different audiences of fifty-five educators rated both the lecture and the lecturer favorably. They were satisfied that they had learned despite irrelevant, conflicting, and meaningless content conveyed in the presentation. Even in the question and answer period, "Doctor Fox" used double talk, neologisms, non sequiturs, and contradictory statements. Almost all the subjects of this experiment were stimulated and satisfied, but they were not educated. See Donald H. Naftulin, John E. Ware, Jr., and Frank A. Donnelly, "The Doctor Fox Lecture: A Paradigm of Education Seduction," *Journal of Medical Education* 48 (July 1973): 630–35.
4. Stephen Cole and Jonathan R. Cole, "Scientific Output and Recognition: A Study in the Operation of the Reward System in Science," *American Sociological Review* 32 (June 1967): 382.
5. David G. Brown, *The Market for College Teachers* (Chapel Hill: University of North Carolina Press, 1965), 146.
6. Ibid., 146–47.
7. It is often argued that publishing is of special value as it is cumulative, it invariably adds to knowledge. However, it should be pointed out that it has been shown that of 10,000 published papers, 100 supply about one-third of the footnotes in other works, and that several thousand are lost or cited so rarely that they do not become generally known. Almost one-third of scientific papers are essentially unnoticed, 10 percent are never cited, another 10 percent are cited once, and 9 percent are cited only twice. Price has shown that on the average, every scientific paper ever published is cited about once a year. As he has noted, scientists have a stronger urge to write papers than to read them. In summing up, he states: "I am tempted to conclude that a very large fraction of the alleged 35,000 journals now current must be reckoned as merely a distant background noise, and as very far from central or strategic in any of the knitted strips from which the cloth of science is woven." Of course, it would be difficult, if not impossible, to separate the dross from what is valuable before work was introduced to the scholarly or scientific community [Derek J. de Solla Price, *Little Science, Big Science...and Beyond* (New York: Columbia University Press, 1986), 62, 73, 105–107, 118].
8. Edward C. Kirkland, "Recipe for Responsibility," *American Association of University Professors Bulletin* 34, (Spring 1948): 23.
9. Francis Bacon, *The Essays; or, Counsels, Civil and Moral* (New York: A. L. Burt, 1883), 244.
10. James Boswell, *The Life of Samuel Johnson*, Vol.I (1709-March 18, 1776) (Bath: George Bayntun, 1925), 305.
11. Noah Porter, *The American Colleges and the American Public* [New York: Arno Press, 1969 (originally published in 1870)], 126.
12. Christopher Jencks and David Riesman, *The Academic Revolution* (Garden City, N.Y.: Doubleday, 1968), 532. It is, of course, somewhat paradoxical to argue that faculty should be engaged in research to improve the quality of their teaching. Research generally takes faculty away from teaching. As a rule, those involved in

research do less undergraduate teaching, and as a result some of it must be done by temporary or part-time faculty who do not do research.

13. See, Ernest L. Boyer, *Scholarship Reconsidered: Priorities of the Professoriate* (Princeton, N.J.: Carnegie Foundation for the Advancement of Teaching, 1990), 23–24.

6

The Concerns of Faculty

The thrust of chapter 3 was that academic life appears to revolve around teaching; it is clearly the professional activity in which the great majority of the professoriate is most involved and what, in turn, most see as their major responsibility. It is the *raison d'etre* and major activity of institutions of higher learning. How this accepted fact manifests itself in some of the broader concerns of faculty is now examined.

Counter to the contention that teaching is at the center of academic life, it seems, at least from the materials reviewed here, that other matters share the attention of academics. When faculty are teaching, it may absorb them; at other times it seems very far from their minds. It is obvious that there is a great deal more to academic life than teaching, and a great deal more in the lives of the professoriate than teaching. There are other matters that capture the attention of academic men and women. The point here is simple and there is no pretense that it is an original insight: when faculty do not have to be mindful of teaching, they are not mindful of it. However, this obvious fact cannot be ignored in ultimately determining how central teaching is to academic life taken as a whole. We review some evidence in the next four chapters.

What Faculty Say

When 210 faculty from seven campuses and a wide range of disciplines were asked in 1992 to enumerate the issues impinging on higher education, those relating to teaching were seldom mentioned. The majority of respondents in this random sample said that they were most anxious about budget cuts, and how these might affect them personally. Specifically, they were most distressed about the possibility of not receiving salary increases or, more troubling, being subject to income reductions or to a policy of short-term give-backs. A considerable number also stated that they were worried about the possibility of being retrenched or losing their fringe benefits. Some found relentless attrition to be as damaging as retrenchment. As more than one put it: "They are letting the department bleed to death."

The respondents had ample opportunity in the lengthy interviews (of about an hour each) to mention any problem that deserved the attention of the academic community. Problems relating to teaching were certainly not overlooked. They were not, however, noted by a large number of respondents; nor when they were registered, were they considered to be particularly important. None were given high priority; those that were specified were, with two exceptions, never listed by more than one in ten respondents. As many as not believed that crowded classrooms and a curtailment in library acquisitions were matters that merited faculty comment. What alarmed many about the former was that the situation could mean heavier teaching loads.

Quite a few expressed dismay about the reduction of funds for professional travel and other perquisites. Only a handful were troubled that a spare budget might result in too few courses to meet undergraduate needs or might add another burden to economically disadvantaged students. Those who were more than moderately apprehensive about the prospect of a reduction of courses were most worried that this could result in the termination of some faculty.

In brief, perspectives were on the whole quite narrow. The future seen by this diverse sample was unquestionably grim: continuing budgetary pressures, downsizing, cutting back on part-time faculty and support staff, larger classes resulting from steady demand combined with diminishing resources, slightly increased teaching loads for some, less money for research in all but a few fields deemed to be in the national interest, and, finally, a continued erosion of support services (recruitment, retention, and placement programs, for example) for students.[1]

To the degree that these responses are typical, the pressures of the 1990s that might directly or indirectly affect teaching are evidently at the fringes of the consciousness of the academic profession. Not surprisingly, they were focused on their own needs. Their attention was most often on material considerations, again hardly surprising during a period of fiscal crisis. The great majority almost never thought about how budgetary problems might affect students. It would be unrealistic, even illusory, to expect otherwise, that faculty would put students before family, career, friendships, and a host of everyday concerns.

Conflict on Campus

We next examined 150 incidents of conflict, most often between faculty and administrators, although sometimes also involving a department chair, an entire peer-review committee, or members of an institution's governing board as a party or respondent, that occurred on American college and university campuses between the middle 1970s and the early 1990s. A number of these events were reported to the American Association of University Professors, which each year is asked to investigate close to one thousand complaints and potential cases.[2] Information about cases was also gathered from formal legal decisions and articles in law reviews and other periodicals and published sources such as campus and community newspapers, *Science*, the *Chronicle of Higher Education*, *Lingua Franca*, and the *New York Times*. Several large stacks of memoranda that invariably fly around academic departments during times of stress were also closely examined, although, given that they are generally circulated by partisans, nothing within these documents was taken at face value.

About half of the cases in the sample ended up in arbitration or in the courts after an appeal to the American Association of University Professors, National Labor Relations Board, United States Equal Employment Opportunity Commission, or some other organization or body. The accumulated reports are quite detailed; only a few lacked pertinent facts, and it was remarkably easy to determine all relevant aspects of a disputation.

It is hardly an overstatement to say that friction on campus—primarily between faculty and academic administrators, but also among faculty and (in universities) between faculty and graduate students—is endemic. It would not have been at all difficult to greatly increase the sample size. At a few institutions, there was only a brief period of calm following the resolution of one incident before another cast a shadow across the campus. At Michigan State University, there were three unrelated episodes that made their way into the sample.

1. A black physician who was denied tenure in the medical school charged that she had not been provided adequate office space, telephone facilities, and secretarial support, and that her work conditions impeded

her ability to carry out her duties in a satisfactory manner. She further claimed that she was inconvenienced because her office was located some distance from others in the department. In addition, she charged that the department head disliked her; her evidence was that he had avoided sitting next to her at faculty meetings. Not only did she have to put up with a lack of resources, but the procedures for evaluating her performance were far from adequate; in fact, they were at best vague. No goals, objectives, or direction had ever been provided so she had no way of knowing how to improve her skills. Taken together, all of this was to her a clear indication of not only being misunderstood and mistreated, but also of blatant racial and sexual discrimination. If she were hired as part of an informal affirmative action program, the institution had an obligation to give her special training and guidance to bring her up to the same standards as others hired through normal processes. Rather than being mentored, she had become a victim of retaliation after she had challenged administrative authorities in the early years of her appointment. The unremitting indignities had made her life miserable.

At the end of her first appointment, she had been recommended for a second three-year term, and at that time she was said to be performing "faithfully and effectively" having "made significant efforts to develop herself as a teacher and as a clinician."

For its part, the administration claimed that she was denied tenure simply because she was still not board certified, was confrontational, abrasive and authoritarian, was not receptive to constructive criticism, and had not been performing her job satisfactorily. It was also noted that she had not been a particularly effective teacher, that she had had more than her share of run-ins with medical students and faculty, and that she had been wanting in carrying out administrative assignments. She was faulted for having failed to show leadership ability. There had certainly been no pattern of discrimination due to race or sex. The court agreed, and the university found her a nonacademic position in the student health center.

2. In another advanced case of grievance, the university had revoked a professor of psychology's tenure after it was learned that he had not told administrative authorities all of the facts surrounding his resignation from his previous position at the University of Toronto. He had in effect been forced to leave after his practitioner's certification had been suspended when it was learned that he had had sexual contact with a

patient. Before he had been hired, he had assured administrative authorities that this was an isolated instance. When more charges were filed against him in Canada, he revealed to the university administration that he had had intimate relations with a number of former patients, and he was immediately fired. He in turn sued on the grounds that he had not been afforded due process. The friction was prolonged when the court ordered the university to reinstate him and grant him a hearing.

3. A distinguished professor of microbiology took action against a number of Michigan State University administrators when he could not get them to exercise their authority to force a graduate student to return his data. She had convinced herself that he intended to steal her work, and those to whom she told her story readily took her side without looking at any evidence or investigating the validity of her accusation. In fact, with their encouragement and assistance, she published a paper from the data, before returning it to an associate dean who had been most instrumental in supporting her actions. He kept the material in his office without informing the professor who had been anxiously awaiting its return, although a number of senior administrators had been told where it was.

Because the microbiologist was not able to continue his work, he was forced to shut down his entire laboratory and this put an end to one of the university's most prominent research programs. He filed a scientific-misconduct charge with the federal government, and after extensive hearings, those administrators who had been involved were faulted for lacking a "demonstrable understanding of the standards of biomedical science," "neglect of evidence, unfounded assumptions, and attribution of malice," and failure to comply with federal regulations. The hearing panel could not understand not only why they did not hand over the data, but why they lent themselves to its publication, and why they did not allow others on the project to become involved in reviewing what the student had written.

Not only at Michigan State University, but around the country, the issues that engage faculty and administrators seem infinite; they range from the trivial to the truly important, and many examples of both types were found. A distinct minority touch on fundamental principles such as the infringement of academic freedom or the denial of due process. The point to remember, however, is that although faculty may be embroiled in a curious range of issues, few of these have anything to do with what they did or did not do in the classroom, or with relationships with undergraduates.

Those that reflect on the performance of an individual are more likely to be about inadequate research productivity or raise questions about someone's shortcomings as a reliable or dependable colleague. Rarely do they revolve around the question of teaching or teaching effectiveness and less often do they even involve students, especially undergraduates. The assignment of courses, how these are taught, what is taught, the complaints of students, academic freedom in the classroom, or the evaluation of course content and teaching are matters about which faculty and administrators very rarely publicly fight. From the data on hand, it would seem that not many faculty are poor teachers, fail to prepare for class, have difficulty getting on with students, do not show enough interest in their courses or students, or are derelict in keeping office hours, advising students properly or in other ways do not meet minimum teaching responsibilities.

The majority of disputes were generated by faculty dissatisfaction over decisions about contract renewals, reappointments, the granting of tenure, promotion decisions, remuneration, and what is perceived by faculty as highhandedness on the part of administrators. There are reports of sexual and racial harassment, egregious and unprofessional retaliation, hostile working environments, and procedural irregularities. There is surely no shortage of issues to create tension on campus. But regardless of how these rifts are categorized, one could only conclude that much of the time teaching is peripheral to the academic enterprise—or, perhaps, that all faculty are seen as adequate teachers, which, while unlikely, could explain why the matter rarely becomes the focus of a dispute.

4. In perhaps the most publicized case of someone denied tenure at the University of California at Berkeley, an assistant professor of mathematics, claiming that the decision was prejudiced, unsuccessfully appealed to various university committees and the administration. She eventually took the matter to court. She had become convinced that those who opposed her appointment were motivated by gender bias: "You asked if there was a subculture antagonistic towards women. I am afraid that the answer is a resounding 'yes.' There are men on the faculty who think that women can't do math." Again: "For ten years, I was treated as a second-class citizen in the U Berkeley math department.... I put my all into that department. But instead of being nurtured and

encouraged, I was faced with obstacles not present for my male peers.... [T]hey changed the promotion rules for me."

After a subcommittee recommended four to one, with one abstention, against her, the Department of Mathematics voted nineteen to twelve, with several abstentions, to deny her tenure. Her reputation was based on two "major results" of her research: Her dissertation, which was concerned with whether jagged motion can be made smooth by looking through an appropriate lens, and a partially completed counter-example for one of the main problems in dynamics and differential topology on which she had been working for a number of years. She had been hired by Berkeley in 1978, three years after earning her Ph.D. Those in the department who made their views known claim that, in the period of eleven years (the tenure vote was taken in 1986), her mathematical accomplishments and promise did not justify awarding her tenure. Although her work was good, the quality was not what it might be, and there was not quite enough. Moreover, not all of her outside evaluations were strong. The—to some— immaterial point was also made that even her best work had had little impact on the field. Many colleagues were convinced that she had been given more than ample time to prove herself.

She next filed a complaint, and a university committee, calling twenty-five witnesses, conducted extensive hearings lasting eighty hours. In the end it concluded that all relevant factors had been considered by the department and that she had not been treated unfairly. Her case was taken up by the media and women's organizations, and was written about in several professional publications such as *Science* and *Notices of the American Mathematical Society*. Among other activities in her public campaign to reverse the department's decision, she testified before state legislators in Sacramento, a congressional committee, and other forums. A number of members of the department of mathematics were portrayed as sexists who used a double standard in assessing her. This, she believed, led to procedural errors. She was portrayed as a victim, as yet another helpless woman.

Over the seven years that the case was publicly debated, teaching was never mentioned by spokespersons for the department of mathematics or the university, and only a few times by the aggrieved professor: "My research was internationally recognized as important, and my publication rate of major works was well within that expected of Berkeley tenured faculty. I ran seminars, turned out my share of Ph.D. students, mentored female graduates and undergraduates, and was a good and popular teacher." A long article in the *Los Angeles Times* describes her as having "scored high in student ratings."

In an effort to compromise, an ad hoc committee of two Berkeley mathematicians, two Berkeley non-mathematicians, and three non-Berkeley mathematicians was appointed to work out a settlement before the case came to trial. It was instructed to focus on whether she presently deserved a tenure appointment at Berkeley. Comparing her with ten men given tenure by the department of mathematics, it concluded that she was better than three, equal to two, and weaker than five. It also judged her to be an above average teacher. It recommended that she be given tenure. In 1993, the chancellor reappointed her to the department as a full professor. After her reinstatement, there was a press conference and press releases, much of which was given front-page coverage by several newspapers. In the swirl of publicity, the focus was almost entirely on alleged improprieties, for example, "a thick glass ceiling"; the matter of teaching was alluded to in the last paragraph of her comments: "...and I look forward to teaching again."

In the materials examined for these many cases, there were, of course, references to such things as negative student evaluations and the teaching of "false doctrines" (e.g., regarding the ordination of women). But these were far less common than conflict that resulted in termination, punishment, or threats due to retrenchment, the elimination of a specific position, the discontinuance of a program (all because of declining enrollments or financial exigency), the abrogation of tenure rights, pressures from ecclesiastical authorities, insubordination, conduct deemed not to be in the best interest of the institution (not being a team player, having poor relations with colleagues, or being divisive), incompetence (sometimes specified, sometimes unspecified), moral turpitude, pressure from public figures, insolence, disruptiveness, a disagreeable manner, an inadequate spirit of cooperativeness or incivility, lacking an appropriate terminal degree, insufficient progress toward a degree (failure to meet educational standards), union activism, and personal or professional unfitness (generally unspecified and unsubstantiated). In most instances, the matter of teaching was at best a secondary concern. In short, an individual stood a far better chance of losing his or her job because of disagreements with or criticisms of a college or university president or some other administrative officer (particularly if these were made public in a newspaper or to a body of sympathetic students or a determined effort was made to bring them to the attention of the governing board) over such issues as authority or policy or for holding inappropriate (e.g., feminist) beliefs or for not holding appropriate (e.g., religious) beliefs.

5. After the Holy See had declared that a professor (who was also a priest) at the Catholic University of America was neither "suitable nor eligible to teach Catholic theology," he asked university authorities that he be permitted to do so. The action by the Vatican was not because of his teaching, but because he had published dissenting views from the teachings of the Catholic church on subjects such as abortion, birth control, and homosexuality. His request was denied, and he was suspended from theological teaching, in effect all teaching, as he was a teacher of theology. The dean of the university's School of Religious Studies and the chair of the department of theology protested any action against the professor. An ad hoc committee of the university's academic senate, acknowledging, as did the professor, that the action against him was within Church law, recommended that he be denied permission to teach only if all aspects of his academic freedom were protected and a place in the university were found for him.

During hearings, the immediate past president of the Catholic Theological Society of America, among others, described his reputation as "very solidly of someone who is in the middle of the road, not...extreme." And a professor from the University of Notre Dame characterized his writing as "squarely within the mainstream of contemporary moral theology." The university administration and the board of trustees rejected the ad hoc committee's recommendation, and insisted that the professor not be permitted to teach Catholic theology in a nonecclesiastical or an ecclesiastical department. All efforts on the part of the professor to negotiate failed:

> I proposed that I move from the department of theology, which has an ecclesiastical faculty, to the department of religion and religious education, which has no ecclesiastical faculty and grants only civil degrees.... And in January of 1987, I offered another compromise whereby I would become a professor-at-large within the university. The compromises I offered then and later were an effort both to ward off potential problems and to keep the academic freedom of CUA [Catholic University of America] intact. If the university itself or any outside church authority forced me to move off the theology faculty and assigned me to religion and religious education or forbade me to teach sexual ethics, academic freedom would have been breached; I could, however, volunteer to do these things without violating the principle of academic freedom. Together with many others, I had worked to gain the

acceptance of academic freedom at CUA, and I wanted to protect that hard-won victory. However, no compromise was accepted. Further, the compromise about not teaching sexual ethics was proposed to the congregation in Rome and rejected.[3]

The professor then filed suit against the university to have his suspension lifted and asked that he be reinstated as a professor of moral theology. The court, asserting that they had a right to side with the Holy See in restricting his teaching, ruled in favor of the administration and board of trustees.

Notwithstanding the sometimes acrimonious debate on so many campuses across the country in recent years over political correctness, the data here indicate that the intensity of conflict over the political slant of teaching and teachers is relatively tame, at least compared to earlier periods. It would appear that few faculty are threatened (or feel threatened enough to complain) because of restrictions on the ideological character of their courses. If they are, such problems are not becoming public. Academic administrators do not seem to be pressuring faculty to follow a particular canon when teaching, and faculty are not reporting feeling pressure. To be sure, if we are to believe a number of national surveys, some of the professoriate feel the need to be more cautious in the classroom than it would like. However, there were no cases in this sample where faculty were punished because their teaching was thought to be politically suspect or tinged. This is in sharp contrast to the 1950s and 1960s when considerable effort was made to keep left-wing ideas out of the classroom.[4]

In a widely publicized incident in 1965–66, for example, a faculty member was dismissed from Adelphi University for introducing too much Marx and Marxism into his courses. The university administration charged him with, among other things, "your restriction of required reading in all three classes to *The Communist Manifesto...*" and went as far as to offer as part of the evidence of what it called his "teaching deficiencies" some examination questions from his courses in introductory sociology, for example :

> The clergy in the middle ages can be likened to: (1) the army of today; (2) the propagandists of today; (3) the secret police of today; (4) all the above; (5) none of the above. [The administration did not provide an answer key.]

The following year at Indiana State University, an instructor of English was fired after he burned a flag on his desk in front of a class.

Before he lit the match he had reminded his students that he was not involved with abstract concepts or questions but with the simple destruction of a concrete object, and what he was doing was not to be misconstrued as an unpatriotic act. Some obviously missed the point.

After the mid-1970s, there was little chance that the misunderstanding of such dramatics would have any consequences. If individuals or organizations are interested in changing the content of what passes as the higher learning they are not acting on it, or are in a position to make faculty feel vulnerable as a result of attempts to do so.

Budgetary considerations, the elimination of faculty positions, or the reorganization of academic programs were by far the most recurrent themes in the pervasive friction on so many campuses in recent years, hardly a surprising finding given concurrent funding cutbacks and the determined pursuit of students and their tuition dollars during this period. The dissension has been primarily about abolishing the rights of tenure or the denial of due process; academic freedom to the degree that it is related to what might have been said in the classroom is seldom an issue. It has been more important to reorganize academic programs or reduce the size of the budget deficit or the faculty and to have everyone acquiesce to this— even those directly and negatively affected by it—by not passing negative judgment and setting aside rights to share in the responsibility of governance than to monitor what students might be learning.

Minorities and women, who are underrepresented among faculty, are overrepresented among those feeling aggrieved; there are many controversies in which they are a party.

6. After the chair of the black studies department at City College of the City University of New York was removed from his administrative position, he sued a number of college officials, alleging violation of his First and Fourteenth Amendment rights of free speech and due process. Just a year earlier he had been unanimously reelected by the department to the post for a three-year term. A jury and then a federal district court judge were convinced that a speech he had given in Albany at the Empire State Black Arts and Cultural Festival was a substantial or motivating factor for the actions taken against him. He was being denied a full three-year term as chair as punishment because his lecture on racial and ethnic biases in the public school curriculum contained derogatory comments about Jews and Italians—for example, that rich Jews had financed the slave trade and that Jews and Italians were involved in a conspiracy

to cause the destruction of blacks by portraying them negatively in films. He referred to one of his critics as an "ultimate, supreme, sophisticated, debonair racist" and "a sophisticated Texas Jew." He also discussed the theory that blacks are benign "sun people" while whites are rapacious "ice people."

Not surprisingly, he and his remarks became the subject of a great deal of media attention. In its defense, acknowledging that the Albany speech was protected by the First and Fourteenth Amendments, the administration countered that it acted mostly because he was sometimes derelict in his duties. Testimony was given stating that he was removed for tardiness in arriving at class and submitting his grade reports. In addition, it noted that his lack of scholarly production had been a factor in its decision. The college added that subsequent to the speech, the professor had been involved in a dispute with another faculty member, that there had been delays in an important faculty search, that there had been deficiencies in monitoring grading, the teaching of classes, and the maintenance of records, that he had failed to attend meetings, and that he had confronted the college president in an inappropriate manner.

None of this was convincing. Indeed, in a memorandum, the dean of social sciences concluded that the professor had met his "ordinary administrative responsibilities...during an extraordinary period of time." The provost also indicated that the professor was adequately carrying out his duties. The administration did add that it believed that the speech would have a negative impact on his and the institution's effectiveness and efficiency. Yet, because there was no evidence that students avoided him or his classes, that alumni fundraising had been hampered, that campus life had been disrupted, that he could not effectively interact with other faculty members, or that the black studies department had become isolated on campus, the court also did not take this argument seriously. The jury found that the Albany speech was a substantial or motivating factor in denying the professor a three-year term as department chair and if he had not said what he had, he would not have been sanctioned. They also concluded that without question he had been deprived of property without due process. (The assumption here seems to have been that the position of chair carries prestige and is a property right.)

The judge suggested that the college might have succeeded if it had shown that the professor "had turned his classroom into a forum for bizarre, shallow, racist, and incompetent pseudo-thinking and pseudo-teaching," which the judge implied should have been made the central issue. Yet, because it had tolerated his teaching for two decades, it could hardly suddenly make the case that it was in fact racist and anti-Semitic. The judge went on to accuse the college of not taking action when it should have, then acting for the wrong reason, and in the end being dishonest about its motivation. The court took the position that while the professor's statements were "hateful, poisonous, and reprehensible," as well as "vulgar [and] repugnant," he had been denied his free speech rights as his talk involved matters of public concern, that merited debate. Punishing him was constitutionally impermissible. He was awarded substantial punitive damages and permitted to continue as chair for the remainder of his term. The judge pointed out that the punitive damages were not a measure of the professor's injury, but a measure of the bad faith of City College. Finally, the college was told that it could monitor his classes and how he performed as chair, and could remove him "from either if a good cause basis for finding abusive or indecent behavior is adequately established."

A court of appeals noted an inconsistency in the jury's findings that school officials were motivated by the "reasonable expectation" that his speech would disrupt effective and efficient operations on campus, while at the same time concluding that they had acted with malicious intent or reckless indifference. The court of appeals vacated the punitive damages and ordered a new trial on this issue. Next the United States Supreme Court granted the college a petition for a writ of certiorari, vacating the judgment and remanding the case to the court of appeals for further consideration. The Supreme Court had recently ruled that the government could fire an employee for disruptive speech based on its reasonable belief of what an employee said, regardless of what was actually said. Moreover, the government employer need only show that the speech is likely to be disruptive before the speaker may be punished, that it threatened to interfere was sufficient grounds. In light of this ruling, the court of appeals reversed itself and held that the professor's First Amendment rights had not been violated since the administration's belief that campus life would be disrupted was reasonable. The entire district court's judgment was reversed. The Supreme Court refused to hear his appeal.

The costs in time, energy, and money in yet another celebrated case about the rights of professors that had absolutely nothing to do with teaching or students was staggering. The entire matter, in fact, is in effect tangential to academic life, more a debilitating quibble about power and personalities than about principles.

More often than not the teaching—or any aspect of the academic performance—of individuals who came to grief was neither cited nor faulted; some of the principals were even recognized and acknowledged as outstanding teachers. In the 10 percent of the disagreements in which it is mentioned, teaching was often a secondary factor; for example, perhaps rooted in what could be called a long-standing domestic quarrel: "Campus issues were discussed, inappropriately, in the classroom." (It was determined that the true issue here was questioning administrative authority.)

Faculty members and administrators found no end of causes to spar over; each believed they had the right to determine what a decorous bulletin board was or to decide whether or not it was proper to place filing cabinets in a hallway. To an outsider the quarrels might seem foolish and all parties petty, but to the combatants the matters were very serious, involving some combination of principle, dignity, rights/responsibilities, or trust.

Even in the not uncommon instances where religious or theological questions were in dispute, it was not likely that the conflict was about what could or could not or had or had not been taught. Disputes began after a faculty member: resigned from a religious order and obtained release from religious vows; was said not to conform to an externally initiated religious test; had remarried in a civil ceremony after a previous Catholic marriage had ended, thirteen years earlier, in civil divorce; was involved in a divorce and was alleged to have acted immorally.

When morality was central, the complaints were due to resistance on the part of faculty to efforts of a president or governing board to reestablish traditional norms or remold an institution to reflect more stringent religious, social, or political views. Most often in these instances individual teachers were not attacked; instead, institutional resources were allocated to change the curriculum. In many cases, more support was given to professional or vocational programs at the expense of the liberal arts.

Teaching as an Issue

In the handful of cases in which teaching played some part in faculty-administrative conflict, there was often a great deal more involved than simply a matter of substandard performance in the classroom. When a faculty member became ensnared in controversy that seemed to touch on his or her teaching, more often than not it was evident that other things were of greater concern to institutional authorities.

7. One worry is that engaging in teaching can be too personal and impassioned. The affirmative action office at the University of Wisconsin at Milwaukee[5] directed that a letter of reprimand be placed in the personnel file of a female professor of English and comparative literature who had been charged with sexual harassment. A well-known feminist teacher and researcher, she had been accused "of depriving women of the opportunity to pursue knowledge." She was said to have violated a campus policy discouraging consensual amorous relations between faculty and students. Two graduate students had accused her of retaliating against them after they had rejected her sexual advances. She had exchanged a kiss in public with one and had pushed the other's rocking chair with a bare foot. The first alleged that the professor made her submit several drafts of a research proposal, while the second saw malice after she refused to provide her with two letters of recommendation.

The professor claimed that her teaching style involved intense and emotional relationships. Flirting and joking with students in order to dispel her authority was part of her pedagogical theory. She added that making students uncomfortable is what teachers must do; it is something quite different from simple erotic behavior. In this case, her actions were misconstrued and the process simply did not work. There may have been a failure on the part of the students to appreciate that one can set high academic standards and yet be casual in everyday encounters outside of the classroom. There was no misconduct on her part, only misunderstanding and hurt feelings. Directly confronting the delicacy of faculty/student relationships, in her appeal the professor wrote:

> Have we decided that students and teachers should not go out to eat together, should not become friends, that it is inappropriate if a student comes to care what a teacher thinks of her? It would be unconscionable to make such a radical change in the nature of education without engaging in extended community discussion.

Her claim that she was not attempting to gain sexual favors and judged her students according to consistent professional standards seemed convincing enough to exonerate her on one count. Although the investigation produced no evidence of unseemly advances or retaliation (she was found not to have discriminated or harassed) in the other case, there was a conclusion that her teaching style was too intense, her pedagogical relations with the first student were too volatile.

8. Another worry involves the possibility of being unfit as a teacher—and as a cooperative faculty member. A tenured professor and former department chair was precipitously terminated from Birmingham-Southern College because of her "long history of ineffectiveness." Not unlike many others, while teaching, she was said to ramble and pursue tangents. In testimony and in written statements, some students praised her classes as stimulating, described her as one of the best teachers at the college, someone easy to talk to, who encouraged discussion and the free expression of ideas. Others found her intimidating, contemptuous, rigid, discouraging, and harsh; they said that they felt forced to withdraw into silence. She was said to curse, yell, and ridicule students, and also to grade unfairly. They felt that she did not respect them or their opinions. There was obviously little agreement as to what kind of teacher she was even among students who were in the same class. There was agreement that she had high standards, expected a great deal from students, was demanding and uncompromising, and gave good grades sparingly. The college was careful to stop at the point of characterizing her as being unfit as a teacher; it was never suggested that she was incompetent. And it was also widely acknowledged that she had very poor relations with the chair of her department, who had replaced her, and with other college administrators. Prior to her dismissal, she had filed four different complaints with the Equal Employment Opportunity Commission; she was accused of verbally abusing, harassing, and showing contempt for colleagues; she took unpopular stands with respect to departmental programs; she was alleged to have advised students to leave the college and enroll elsewhere; and it was reported that she frequently and publicly failed to show respect for the opinions of colleagues. It is quite obvious, and was not denied by campus authorities, that having offended so many powerful people on campus was as much a factor in her dismissal as her deficiencies as a teacher.

9. Then there is the issue of unintelligibility. When Morehouse College, which is predominantly black, did not renew the contract of an associate professor of physics who had been born in China, he filed a complaint with the Equal Employment Opportunity Commission that he had been the victim of discrimination. He also sued the college for

injunctive relief, reinstatement, back pay, and damages. Because he had been told by the chair of his department that only blacks could expect advancement at the college, there was no doubt in his mind that the only issue was discrimination: "What I base it on is based on my feeling. And I asked the government to find out about it." His English and teaching, which had been personally evaluated by the college president and three successive department chairs, were said to be insufficient to justify retention. Students agreed that he was completely ineffective in the classroom. The president testified that the decision to terminate was due to the professor's "deficiency in oral and written language skills" and his "teaching ineffectiveness." He claimed that in thirty years of administrative work he had never seen such negative teaching evaluations. He had had considerable experience teaching English around the world and he had not encountered anyone as weak orally. He criticized the professor's usage, grammar, sentence structure, and idioms. He felt that he was a particularly poor example for the college's students, who had serious language problems of their own. The college prevailed.

Notwithstanding this last example, substandard teaching by itself was seldom the issue precipitating conflict on campus. Much more often it is someone's inexplicable and bizarre behavior.

From time to time, but truly very rarely, a widely recognized and popular teacher is terminated. When this occurs, the inevitable outcry from sympathetic colleagues and students and the subsequent publicity in the media creates a perception that such incidents happen more often than they actually do.

10. In 1992, the Department of Political Science at Duke University voted eight to six (with one abstention) not to recommend an assistant professor for tenure. There was little question that he was a fine teacher; he was said to have an "infectious interest" in both teaching and research. He routinely earned high ratings in the *Teacher-Course Evaluation Book* published for students. One of his courses was among the most popular and largest at Duke. He had been nominated more than once for the Duke Alumni Undergraduate Teaching Award. Here is how his teaching was described in the student newspaper:

> On Wednesday, [he] was teaching his trademark international relations course. Gripping his podium, leaning forward and raising his voice...told 150 students that Shakespeare's *Macbeth* provides a perfect example of how people view power.

"We focus on it negatively. Power is evil," he said. "But power can also be a force for good." [He] used this idea to segue into a lecture on the dynamics and definitions of power. His lectures echoed other lectures he had given to the class.

He jotted an outline on the blackboard for students to copy, he paced the stage using hand gestures to emphasize his points and cracked a couple of jokes. Even though the class was in Griffith Film Theater, [he] did not need a microphone to be heard. He reminded his class to sign-up to have lunch with him for the following Monday.

Drawing on examples from saints fighting dragons to Desert Storm battles, [he] illustrated the points he made. Most of the students listened attentively even though it's a 9:10 a.m. class.

"You don't look at your watch in this class," said Trinity freshman Erik Johnson.

Over 900 students signed a petition supporting his bid for tenure, and concerned alumni wrote letters. There was a call for an outside evaluation by disinterested scholars. There were a number of appeals and reviews, each resulting in considerable publicity. The university president evaluated his work and planned to recommend tenure, but was prevented from doing so by university bylaws. The provost turned him down three times. A faculty hearing committee found procedural faults and recommended that the case be reconsidered. The chair of the executive committee of the board of trustees was assured by the university counsel that this would occur: "The committee has recommended, and the provost has agreed, that [his] candidacy for tenure will be completely reevaluated by the provost and his advisory promotion and tenure committee. The provost will recommend that a special ad hoc committee be appointed to consider all information (including recently developed manuscripts and viewpoints of the Yale [University] Press) relevant to the matter. At the end of the day the process will result in a positive or negative decision by the provost. There is no question that this reevaluation will be fair, complete, and comprehensive. You and I know that [the provost] is capable of no less." The review was not undertaken. A final appeal was ultimately rejected by the executive committee of the board of trustees. The outcome was less significant than the fact that his petition to the board of trustees made no mention of teaching.

[The] principal contention...is simple: in the review...of 1992, the Appointment, Promotion, and Tenure Committee ("AP&T") and the provost (1) failed to conduct a meaningful evaluation of his completed, revised book manuscript... which was properly in his dossier at the time of their reviews but was *never* evaluated and (2) failed to apply procedures which were intended to assure that his scholarship, including the revised and completed manuscript, received adequate and proper consideration by failing to make inquiry of his department or school, or of outside evaluators, to assess the significance of the revised, completed manuscript.... From the beginning, [the] principal desire in pursuing his appeal has been to obtain an objective evaluation of his scholarship which takes into consideration the particular character of his subspecialty, security studies, takes account of his interdisciplinary scholarship, and gives adequate consideration of his most recent scholarship as manifested in the revised, completed book manuscript which was not evaluated in a meaningful way in his tenure review. At pages 6-8 of his grievance to the university ombudsman he proposed the constitution of a panel of scholars to evaluate his candidacy free of "factional discrimination and personal bias" in his department and the history and "publicity and attendant pressures" on the AP&T.

In its thirty-seven-page report, the special committee of the executive committee of the board of trustees quickly passed over his teaching, and moved on to the single issue of concern: "He is acknowledged to be an excellent teacher who has also contributed to the university. These criteria, however, are not sufficient to grant tenure; outstanding academic scholarship is critical, and it is in this area that [his] tenure review was problematic. Despite the grant of an additional year to finish the manuscript that was central to his tenure decision, [he] did not complete it in a timely fashion. Moreover, the reviews of what had been completed—both by evaluations inside and outside of Duke—were mixed."

The university's contention was that the case had been given ample "substantive and procedural" review, making it controversial, complicated, and confusing. And at each turn the controversy, complications, and confusion was detailed in the press. Some who did not support the granting of tenure were accused of having done so out of vindictiveness or pettiness. They were said to be offended by his "outspokenness," by the political slant of his scholarship in that he seemed to be an apologist for the American involvement in the Vietnam War, by his failure to utilize statistical techniques in his research, by the fact that he was a former army intelligence officer, by his use of what they perceived to be outdated theories.

The counterclaim was made that he was rejected for purely professional reasons; the decision had nothing to do with methodology, personality, or ideology. According to the Duke faculty handbook, outstanding scholarship is an "indispensable qualification" for tenure. One of his colleagues acknowledged that with three published books and a lengthy, nearly completed manuscript, he "generally had the number of pages required for tenure.... The question was the quality of the pages when it was clear they weren't terrible. Was the quality good enough for Duke?" He chose not to do research on the "frontiers" of his field and "when outsiders in international relations were asked to rank him with other people of his generation in international relations, he tended to be off the scope." In other words, letters from others in the discipline assessing his scholarship raised questions about its significance. It was also pointed out that one of his books was based on his dissertation, and that a strong dissertation does not guarantee tenure. Another colleague added that his two other books, while good, were not significant contributions to his field. The standards may have been high, but they were fair.

The provost noted that Duke's department of political science "has a chance to be in the top tier of departments in the United States. Every tenure decision will help push it to that top tier." His contention was that if the university wanted to maintain its high level of excellence, it must settle for nothing less than outstanding research. Good research and excellent teaching would not help a department increase its prestige and visibility. Many in the department believed that academic standards needed to be improved, that it needed to become more selective when granting tenure. Shifting and uncertain standards may cause pain, it was argued, but this was a necessary price in order to attract the very best graduate students who ultimately would find desirable academic positions.

This incident, and others like it, even if relatively uncommon, raises questions about the weight of teaching in tenure decisions. The role given to research is incomprehensible to nonacademics—and many academics. Why should research count for so much and teaching count for so little? As the principal in this last case put it: "That's the real tragedy of this, that the students weren't heard, that the teaching dimension to the profession is an invisible cloak at the time of tenure. It's the very visible cloak that every one of us wears every day. Students don't see us as researchers, they see us as teachers, and that cloak disappears completely at the tenure time."

It is not so much a lack of agreement about an individual's worth as about what academics should value that leads to the protracted rancor when a committed teacher is denied tenure. The charges and immediate denials over a long period of time not only add to everyone's discomfort, but leave the impression that those who care about teaching are at risk.

This is not the case. If academics skirmished less about symbols and more about such issues, those on and off campus might reach a better understanding of why departments in search of greater prestige and visibility put themselves through such distress, even if only infrequently.

We now turn to what academics say about themselves and their colleagues.

Notes

1. Lionel S. Lewis and Philip G. Altbach, "The True Crisis on Campus," *Academe* 80 (January/February 1994): 24–25.
2. Of the total reported to the American Association of University Professors, the greatest number are allegations, not acted on as cases; over 20 percent are closed, one-tenth or more following successful mediation by the Association's staff.
3. Charles E. Curran, *Catholic Higher Education, Theology, and Academic Freedom* (Notre Dame, Ind.: University of Notre Dame Press, 1990), 212.
4. Lionel S. Lewis, *Cold War on Campus: A Study of the Politics of Organizational Control* (New Brunswick, N.J.: Transaction Publishers, 1988).
5. Sexual harassment was at the center of a case at the same institution a decade earlier. An assistant professor of occupational therapy who was denied tenure filed suit alleging sexual discrimination and sexual harassment. The assistant dean of her school had made suggestive comments and was aggressive in other ways. "He repeatedly leered...and would...touch her, rub up against her, place objects between her legs, make suggestive remarks and comments about various parts of her body." He ignored requests that he not treat her in this manner, but his advances became more brazen, culminating in an assault at a Christmas party. There he followed her into the bathroom, where he told her that "he had to have her" and that "he would have her." He forcibly kissed and fondled her, but was interrupted by her boyfriend. There were no sexual overtures for the next fifteen months, but shortly before the hearing on the renewal of her contract he falsely accused her of misusing the university's photocopying equipment. After she was cleared of the charges, she was reappointed.

   The district court found that the assistant dean was guilty of sexual harassment, and that his actions created an abusive working environment in violation of the law. The assistant dean argued that his actions resulted from sexually driven desire, and, therefore, were not sex-based harassment. She was a member of a class with whom he desired to have an affair. The court rejected this argument. He finally claimed that he harbored no hatred of the protected class (women). In rejecting this tack, the circuit court stated: "All that is required is that the action taken be motivated by the gender of the plaintiff. No hatred, no animus, and no dislike is required." At the same time, the court rejected her allegations that the director of the occupational therapy program subjected her to salary and workload disparities, unprecedented student evaluations, poor appraisals, mistreatment at faculty meetings, limited research time, retaliation for exercise of her First Amendment rights, and interference in the tenure process. She was not awarded tenure.

7

Defining Merit

There is no more common watchword in academe than *merit*. In colleges and universities, appointments, promotions, tenure, salary increases, and ultimately reputations are said to depend on it. How is merit defined? What do academics mean by merit? When it is said that someone has merit, what specific qualities is the academic profession talking about—excellence in teaching, research, service, or some combination of two or all three? Surely, if teaching is as significant among the various academic roles performed by faculty as the two other major functions, research (publication or creative achievements) and service, then it should be as pivotal as these in the definition of merit. This matter is now considered.[1]

The Data

In an effort to understand what academics have in mind when they speak of merit, a selection of letters of recommendation justifying merit salary increases for faculty was examined. The letters are from a large, fairly typical, northeastern, respected but not venerated, public university center.[2] They cover merit salary increases for all faculty members, except those in the health sciences, for two successive years. There was a total of 417 requests, of which 408 were successful.[3]

A qualitative and quantitative analysis of the letters (which were from one paragraph to several pages)—written by the candidates themselves, by senior faculty (mostly department chairs), and by administrators (mostly deans), spelling out why a merit salary increase was deserved—was undertaken in order to isolate the qualities of job performance that were valued. Three-sevenths of the nominations were written by a departmental chair; a little over one-fourth were written by a dean; and a little less than one-fourth were written by the candidates themselves. About 10 percent of the self-nominations carried a chair's or another administrator's endorsement, and about the same number of the chair's nominations carried a dean's endorsement, most of which merely reiterated the main points made in the original statement. Before categories for coding were formulated, close to 10 percent of the documents were perused. A fifty-five-item code book was developed, and the data was classified using standard techniques of content analysis.[4]

Over 80 percent of the recommendations were for males, and fewer than 20 percent were for females. Over 40 percent of the nominees were full professors; slightly less than 40 percent were associate professors; 14 percent were assistant professors; and 5 percent were lecturers or instructors. The most prominently represented faculty division was arts and letters with 29 percent of the nominations; the faculty of natural sciences and mathematics was represented with 21 percent; social sciences with 14 percent; educational studies with 10 percent; engineering with 7 percent; and the faculties of management, law, and the other professions with less than 5 percent each. These figures are consistent with the distribution of full-time faculty at the institution, except that full professors and those from arts and letters are overrepresented, while faculty from the social sciences are notably underrepresented.

The amount of the merit salary increase requested was generally modest, although such awards are not one-year bonuses, but increases in base salary, the effects of which are cumulative. The amounts actually awarded reflected the amounts requested fairly closely; less than 3 percent received more than was asked for, and 10 percent received less than was requested. There were 232 awards conferred in the first round, and 176 in the second round. Sixty-nine individuals were selected both times.

How Important Is Teaching?

Roughly two-thirds of the letters referred to student contacts, mentioning excellence (e.g., "effective," "successful," "solid") in teaching (37 percent), academic and nonacademic advisement, generally graduate (34 percent), enrollments or teaching load (19 percent), the development of a new course (17 percent), service in pivotal or crucial courses (15 percent), activity in the development of departmental curriculum

(10 percent), and popularity with students (7 percent). More recommendations in which the matter of teaching was raised touched on just one of these aspects (28 percent) than on two (22 percent), three (13 percent), or four or five (7 percent).

> He willingly and ably taught...last year because we had a special need...even though he had not taught the course for several years, and was presently concentrating both his teaching and scholarship in the field of....

> The results of all of the...teaching evaluations have shown him to be a conscientious, well prepared instructor, who demands excellence of his students. The courses he teaches have substance and depth, and all students respect him for that.

> He is an excellent teacher, well organized and prepared and liked by his students. For these reasons he was appointed director of undergraduate studies last January.

A similar message was conveyed in letters of self-nominees:

> I carry as heavy a real teaching load as any faculty member in the department. Every semester my classes—both graduate and undergraduate—are filled and I have many requests to force register students. Students regularly take second and third classes with me. Many former students ask if they can sit in on classes they have had before. Even though I've never received a teaching award from this university, the students have consistently voted with their presence.

Only about 40 percent of these recommendations were augmented with some evidence—a reference to a particular course, formal or informal student evaluations, enrollment figures, the names of student advisees, a general statement that "course reviews had been good," and the like:

> Recently he has been involved in the senior/junior...laboratory, where he functioned not only as the instructor of record, but performed the duties of the teaching assistant when the assigned T/A was suspended from the university early in the semester.

> [He] has assumed a major role in developing one of our important graduate courses and has been recognized as a good teacher.

> [He] developed two new courses...and taught them on overload, one each semester. The courses serve our minority students.

How Important Is Research?

Research, publication, or creative achievements was cited in 73 percent of the letters. Most prominently mentioned here was peer recognition, participation in professional meetings, obtaining a research grant, or some activity in a professional organization. In about three-quarters of these cases a count of publications, a listing of journals, the name of a funding agency, or the size of a grant was included.

> She has managed to participate in scholarly conferences and has had an article accepted for publication.

> [He] has completed a major manuscript on the history of the...movement that is presently under consideration at several [journals].

> His publication record includes...books, and a steady output of articles and reviews each year. He serves not only as an associate editor of...but carries the brunt of the editorial work on a...series...sources for students...which he co-edits.

> Since last spring he has had four of his accepted papers now published, and has one more in the galley proof stage, and has as well two more substantial papers (thirty and twenty-four ms. pages) newly accepted. In June he was an invited speaker.... For us...represents precisely the type of active researcher in...that the department is trying to attract *and keep*. He clearly deserves a very substantial merit increase at this time.

Supporting the dark criticism of academic life that what one publishes is less important than how much one publishes, in these documents quantity is more widely recognized than quality. Quality (often indicated by the number of times a candidate's work had been cited or reprinted) was specified in 29 percent of the letters, while quantity was specified in about twice as many, 57 percent. (However, it is worth noting that the size of the salary increase requested and received for the former was greater than for the latter.)

Other aspects of research mentioned were recognition (21 percent), participation in professional meetings (26 percent), obtaining a research grant (27 percent), doing some professional work such as being on the editorial board of a professional journal or having a leadership role in a professional organization (15 percent), and being visible to other scholars or scientists—being renowned or receiving invitations to speak to others—(28 percent).

How Important Is Service?

Four-fifths of the recommendations used service—such as committee or administrative work—as the rationale for a merit salary increase. Half of these mentioned at least two administrative chores or committee assignments in which the candidate was involved. Departmental administrative work was referred to twice as often as divisional or institutional administrative work, but work on departmental, divisional, and institutional committees received equal mention.

The letters were generally quite specific with regard to service; a particular task was mentioned in over 85 percent of the recommendations in which institutional service was touched upon. But, as in the cases of teaching and research, rarely was there any proof that candidates performed meritoriously, only that they performed. The following excerpts are typical:

> There is no need, I am sure you will agree, to recount here the professional accomplishments and long and extraordinary service of Professor...to this university. He is a scholar of national repute and a very gifted teacher. If his output in these areas fell in the last few years (fell, that is, relative to his own very high output) it was only because he devoted so much of his enormous energy to the tasks that came to him in his administrative capacity or that he was asked to assume by other levels of the university administration.

> In our department, there is no faculty member so widely known and respected for the consistency of his university service as Professor.... As the appended recent supplement to his Vita demonstrates, he is constantly requested for service on various and important university search committees, most recently the search for....

> He has also planned a...institute to serve greater, a clearing house for....

> Professor...has performed admirably during her first year as chairman [sic].... Not only has she been able to maintain the high level of administrative efficiency which we have come to expect from that department, but she has also been instrumental in bringing a new program into the department....This should have a significant positive effect on...enrollments. In the councils of the faculty [her] voice has come to be recognized and respected. Her contributions have been characterized by the kind of clarity of vision and intelligent rigor that have always been associated with her scholarship.

Recommendations that touched on matters other than teaching, research, or administrative activities showed that faculty who were perceived as being dependable ("diligent"), energetic ("dynamic"), hard-working ("vigorous"), valuable, and willing to take on extra work were deemed especially deserving of a merit salary increase. Nothing comes in for more praise than being a "stabilizing force," a "positive role model," or possessing "needed leadership qualities." A few letters alluded to a candidate's skills in interpersonal relations, and most that did were written by deans.

Letters were classified according to the activity that was most heavily emphasized. To a certain extent, this is in part a subjective measure. It includes an assessment of the amount of attention given to teaching, research, or service tasks; the number of points raised with regard to each activity; and the amount of evidence to support various assertions. Each letter was also classified according to the relative emphasis (i.e., strong, moderate, none) placed on teaching, research, and service.

Whereas teaching was strongly emphasized in 28 percent of the letters while not mentioned in 31 percent, and research was strongly emphasized in 52 percent of the letters and not mentioned in 27 percent, institutional service was strongly emphasized in 56 percent of the letters while not mentioned in only 18 percent. Furthermore, academic criteria (i.e., teaching, research, or a combination of the two) weighed most heavily for only one-third of the recommendations, whereas for the remainder, service, was emphasized just as much or more. Moreover, the more attention given to administrative effort, the larger the recommended salary increase.

The letters written by a department chair generally emphasized administrative activities more than research,[5] while those written by the candidates themselves were just as likely to emphasize research accomplishments. The chairs' nominations took more notice of teaching activities—excellence, service, enrollments, advisement—than did nominations initiated by deans or by the candidates themselves. Deans were most concerned with administrative or committee work, particularly management tasks outside the candidate's department, and gave little attention to other matters. Many simply ignored subjects such as research quality, research quantity, and research recognition. Efforts and success in the classroom were not often mentioned by anyone but candidates themselves.

Additional analysis of the letters reveals that the arguments put forth for merit salary increases were related to a nominee's gender, rank, and academic discipline. There are clear and consistent differences between the recommendations for higher-status and for lower-status individuals, which in turn suggests a hierarchy of the most- and least-valued academic activities.[6]

Letters for women cited teaching more frequently than research (28 percent versus 17 percent), whereas letters for men were more likely to focus on their research over teaching (38 percent versus 17 percent). Likewise, the proportion of recommendations that focused most heavily on contributions to the teaching program declined with increasing rank—lecturers or instructors, 46 percent; assistant professors, 21 percent; associate professors, 20 percent; full professors, 14 percent. Nearly one-half of the letters for lecturers or instructors emphasized teaching most heavily, while only about one-eighth of those for full professors did so. For the lower ranks, more cases were made on the basis of special service in teaching, the development of new courses, and working on the departmental curriculum. A statement about meritorious teaching was the first criterion mentioned in twice as many recommendations for lecturers, instructors, or assistant professors as for full professors (28 percent versus 15 percent). At the same time, research accomplishments (quality, quantity, recognition, and professional work and visibility) were most heavily emphasized in the letters for over 40 percent of the full professors; this was the case for only one of the twenty-two lecturers and instructors.

Compared to those in other disciplines, the recommendations for scientists depended least on nonacademic arguments and were more likely to emphasize primarily research, and to a lesser degree teaching contributions. Scientists were also more likely to support their assertions with evidence. They rarely reverted to platitudes (3 percent compared to 20 percent for both social scientists and arts and letters faculty).

> I would like to recommend Dr.... for a merit salary increase of...per year. He has during this past year developed several ingenious experiments which broaden considerably our understanding of problems related to energy.

For their part, social scientists paid more attention to nonacademic contributions to campus life such as departmental administrative service, so that their letters not only strongly emphasized these activities, but provided examples of such work as supporting evidence a remarkable 94 percent of the time. Although eager to cite examples of administrative work, they were vague when describing teaching.

In the end, the largest merit salary increases went to the scientists; 27 percent of them received one of the larger increases, while this was true for less than 4 percent of the social scientists.

Overall, it appears that participation in administrative or committee functions is more important for a merit salary increase than either teaching or research activities. Moreover, teaching seems to be less valued than not only administrative service, but also than research. It was somewhat of a surprise how highly valued institutional service is in the contemporary university. It may not quite be a *sine qua non* for academic success, but it is without question an essential factor in the definition of academic merit. This does not appear to be the case for teaching. This conclusion is reinforced when we consider the size of a merit salary increase in relation to the various issues raised in a nominating letter.

When factors such as research quantity, recognition, professional visibility, and the like are mentioned, or when research was simply emphasized more heavily in a recommendation, this had a perceptible and positive effect on the amount of a merit salary increase. Letters in which research was the most heavily emphasized criterion were less likely to result in one of the smaller salary increases than those in which teaching was the most heavily emphasized subject (11 percent versus 37 percent). At the same time, 22 percent of those letters extolling research received one of the larger merit salary increases, while this was so for only 10 percent with inordinate praise for teaching.

Merit salary increases for individuals whose letters did not mention research activities averaged 20 percent less than the mean award. Even moderate emphasis on research accomplishments had an effect of increasing an award to above the mean. The more emphasis on service, the larger the merit salary increase. However, heavy emphasis on teaching was related to a smaller award than when it was not mentioned, or only mentioned in passing.

Finally, the results of a statistical analysis to determine what factors increase or decrease the size of a merit salary award indicated that recipients of large increases were more likely to have a greater number of references to research and administrative service in their letters, to be female, and to hold high academic rank. Those who received the smallest awards were more likely to be social scientists and to have a greater number of references to teaching in their letters.

The analysis of these recommendations goes well beyond reaffirming the commonplace that research is valued more than teaching. The letters reveal a set of priorities favoring administrative or committee functions over traditional academic pursuits. The impression one is left with is that the pressures on university faculty are not from research, that it is not the urgency of publishing or perishing that keeps them from giving attention to students. It would appear that to be seen as meritorious, faculty are primarily expected to be part-time administrators or bureaucrats.[7]

How Mathematicians Define Merit

These findings are unexceptional. A very different source of data, a national survey of a sample of mathematicians, makes it readily apparent that these requests for merit salary increases pretty closely reflect how merit is generally defined by American academics, and is indicative of the relative centrality given to research and service compared to teaching across the country. (For a range of comparable figures, see the appendix to this chapter.)

A survey of 476 department chairs and 1008 faculty members completed by the Joint Policy Board for Mathematics in 1992-93[8] found that most agreed that research should be of greatest importance in merit salary increases. However, for most other activities—classroom teaching, service to the institution, service to the profession, service to the local community, interdisciplinary research involving new mathematics, application of existing mathematics to other fields, research on educational issues, presenting colloquium and seminars, expository writing, student advising, doctoral thesis supervision, master's and bachelor's thesis supervision, and curriculum development—the percentage who said that any one should be an important factor was greater than those who said that it already was. In the top-ranked doctorate-granting departments, 50 percent of the faculty believe that teaching actually is important in determining merit salary increases, and over 90 percent believe that it should be; just under 50 percent believe that service to the institution is important in determining merit salary increases, and just over 70 percent believe that it should be.

The percent of faculty who believe that teaching is and should be important is naturally greater in less research-oriented institutions. About 90 percent of the faculty from institutions which only offer a bachelor's degree in mathematics believe that teaching is important and close to 100 percent believe that it should be important in merit salary increases. Not as many believe that service is and should be important.

Faculty strongly favored rewarding people for excellence in this area [educational responsibilities] and felt equally strongly that under the current system this is not done as much as it should be. There was a high degree of consensus that these responsibilities include not only classroom presentation but also advising, consulting with students outside of class, preparing syllabi and tests, creating instructional materials such as software and visual aids, developing curricula, and the like.[9]

Between one-fifth to one-third of faculty in doctoral-granting departments are convinced that teaching has become more valued in determining merit salary increases than in the recent past, while almost equal numbers in departments that grant master's or bachelor's degrees are convinced that it has become less valued.

In sum, the materials gathered and reviewed here indicate that what the academic world understands as merit embodies three basic factors—research, service, and teaching. Teaching may not be paramount, but it is certainly not inconsequential. What others describe as outstanding teaching can at times be a sufficient condition to presume merit. As with the case of service, at times it may not be a necessary condition.

How much teaching is valued by the professoriate is also the subject of the next chapter. The focus, what is known and said about the teaching of academics hoping to advance their careers, is much like that of this chapter. The data are letters of recommendation written for job candidates. We are interested in what academics believe should be weighed in evaluating and acting on individuals in the labor market.

Notes

1. The question of how meritocratic academic life truly is will not be addressed here as it is an entirely different problem and has been the subject of an earlier study. See Lionel S. Lewis, *Scaling the Ivory Tower: Merit and Its Limits in Academic Careers* (Baltimore, Md.: Johns Hopkins University Press, 1975).

2. Obviously, it is very likely that a sample of merit salary requests from another type of institution such as a comprehensive college would look quite different, and it would be risky to generalize the findings reported in this chapter to campuses where there are different expectations for faculty. The evaluation system at some institutions where it is understood that faculty must both teach and publish leaves little doubt that the former is more peripheral in the assessment of merit. Examples were found where, when faculty were formally evaluated, equal points were given for winning a teaching award and publishing a journal article. This number was considerably smaller than what was awarded for writing a book. Those who could not show evidence of a viable research program risked sanctions even if their teaching was satisfactory or better. To underline the point, a department chair wrote: "Good teaching and service cannot substitute for scholarship."

   To many, the following examples from the published merit point system from a social sciences department at Bowling Green State University may seem absurd, but they are not atypical of the thinking and actions of faculty and administrators around the country:

Activity	Points
Article in one of the two leading disciplinary journals	25
Article in a medium "impact" journal	15

Book (prestige monograph) written for peers	25-30
Book chapter	5-8
Submission of proposal to national agency/foundation	5-10
Receipt of grant/contract from national agency	20-25
Receipt of grant/contract, state/local	2-10
Highest evaluation category for each course taught	3
New course development	8
Taught large class (190+ students)	5
Master Teacher nomination	1
Master Teacher award	25
Elected office in national professional organization	6
Department ad hoc committee assignment	1-4

3. It is unclear of why such a high percentage of nominations succeeded. It is possible that institutional mechanisms exist that discourage unlikely candidates for a merit salary increase from applying for one, or that those applications that failed to win endorsement at any one administrative level vanished into some fathomless file drawer, or that nearly all applications for merit salary increases are commonly approved. Whatever the case, after several intensive searches it was evident that these records were the most complete and available.

4. Most coding, such as determining rank or discipline, was straightforward and simple; some, such as ascertaining what was most heavily emphasized in a recommendation, demanded more attention.

5. The defense for giving priority to administrative over academic work was set forth by the chair of the Department of English in a memorandum to his colleagues addressing the shortage of funds in the distribution of merit money in 1994:

> The department was given $7,000 in this round. All of this was designated for administrative salary debts that went back in some cases to 1991. There is still further unresolved indebtedness for administrative salaries for last year.... One particular burden which puts stress on both $50,000 pools is a series of obligations negotiated by previous deans with A&L [Arts and Letters] chairs for the payment of merit money for administrative service. These claims are considerable and compete at the decanal level with faculty claims for academic merit.... All of us would agree that faculty administrators must be compensated. The size of the department makes the jobs proportionally complex and time-consuming, distracting significant time and energy from teaching and scholarship.... I was concerned with stabilizing administrative stipends while at the same time freeing all of the designated merit money for its originally intended purpose. I am convinced, as are many others, that economic conditions are **not** going to improve; it is entirely possible that discretionary funds might again become unavailable, jeopardizing administrative stipends if they should stay in that category. I will continue to press for such stipends as additions to base, as should my successors."

6. It is possible, of course, that meritorious performance may vary within any one of these three categories so that, for example, females may be seen to be better teachers than males. We can do no more than take note of this likelihood, since there is no way of knowing with this sample of letters whether this is the case.

7. The move toward bureaucracy, which institutions of higher learning appear to be inexorably following, may ironically stem from the increased emphasis on aca-

demic research. As scholarly specialization occurred over this century, decision-making power regarding personnel (e.g., recruitment and promotion) and the conditions of the workplace (e.g., curriculum and teaching load) shifted from the central administration to the divisional and departmental levels. This elaborate layering of bureaucratic structure opened up alternative avenues for faculty career advancement. As the changes have taken hold, the mission of higher education may have been inadvertently supplanted by organizational forces that press for increasingly greater attention to institutional process at the expense of research and teaching.

8. *Recognition and Rewards in the Mathematical Sciences,* Report of the Joint Policy Board for Mathematics, Committee on Professional Recognition and Rewards (Washington, D.C.: American Mathematical Society, 1994). (See also, Supplementary Data Report, Section B. Selected Data.)

9. Ibid., 7.

Appendix: How Mathematicians Define Merit

Questions: How important for merit salary increases do you think each of the following activities (actually is? = I) (should be? = S)

Type of Institution

	Top-ranked doctorate granting	Next-ranked doctorate granting	Not-ranked doctorate granting	Master's degree granting	Bachelor's degree granting
			(percent responding "very important")		
Research in the discipline:					
I (faculty)	97	89	88	62	32
I (chairs)	100	100	93	65	32
S (faculty)	91	86	86	67	41
S (chairs)	97	95	97	62	33
Classroom teaching:					
I (faculty)	8	14	24	50	62
I (chairs)	29	51	53	74	83
S (faculty)	36	51	63	78	92
S (chairs)	48	76	75	92	98
Institutional service:					
I (faculty)	3	2	4	16	28
I (chairs)	7	8	7	19	33
S (faculty)	13	8	8	23	29
S (chairs)	17	11	15	23	36
Professional service:					
I (faculty)	3	2	3	6	4
I (chairs)	0	5	0	4	8
S (faculty)	7	5	7	12	13
S (chairs)	4	13	5	11	12
Service as a mathematician to the community:					
I (faculty)	1	1	2	7	5

Type of Institution (continued)

	Top-ranked doctorate granting	Next-ranked doctorate granting	Not-ranked doctorate granting	Master's degree granting	Bachelor's degree granting
		(percent responding "very important")			
I (chairs)	0	3	0	11	5
S (faculty)	7	9	9	19	13
S (chairs)	4	16	7	21	14
Interdisciplinary research involving new math:					
I (faculty)	28	36	31	31	12
I (chairs)	60	57	55	31	14
S (faculty)	51	58	49	44	25
S (chairs)	54	67	66	40	24
Applications of existing math to other fields:					
I (faculty)	14	11	15	17	7
I (chairs)	36	35	28	21	10
S (faculty)	25	35	32	33	23
S (chairs)	32	44	38	29	22
Research on educational issues:					
I (faculty)	4	3	6	12	9
I (chairs)	9	13	11	13	5
S (faculty)	10	9	21	22	17
S (chairs)	15	31	25	21	18
Presenting papers at conferences:					
I (faculty)	17	12	13	27	16
I (chairs)	7	14	16	29	24
S (faculty)	14	17	17	20	18
S (chairs)	13	21	13	26	20
Presenting colloquiums and seminars:					
I (faculty)	12	11	8	11	7
I (chairs)	4	11	8	18	17
S (faculty)	13	14	14	17	15
S (chairs)	11	21	12	16	17
Expository writing:					
I (faculty)	2	2	6	6	7
I (chairs)	0	11	0	6	5
S (faculty)	8	9	16	15	11

Type of Institution (continued)

	Top-ranked doctorate granting	Next-ranked doctorate granting	Not-ranked doctorate granting	Master's degree granting	Bachelor's degree granting
			(percent responding "very important")		
S (chairs)	11	19	8	17	15
Student advising:					
I (faculty)	3	2	4	8	16
I (chairs)	4	8	2	16	8
S (faculty)	9	13	11	17	27
S (chairs)	7	11	10	22	32
Dissertation supervision:					
I (faculty)	25	17	25	na	na
I (chairs)	25	51	40	na	na
S (faculty)	48	45	44	na	na
S (chairs)	66	63	63	na	na
Master's and bachelor's thesis supervision:					
I (faculty)	1	1	7	10	6
I (chairs)	0	3	11	13	14
S (faculty)	3	12	17	22	17
S (chairs)	26	9	22	20	19
Curriculum development:					
I (faculty)	4	4	3	7	12
I (chairs)	4	3	7	17	19
S (faculty)	15	16	19	24	30
S (chairs)	21	11	28	34	32
Competing offers from other institutions:					
I (faculty)	75	54	32	9	12
I (chairs)	86	47	33	8	4
S (faculty)	21	16	10	9	4
S (chairs)	59	31	21	4	0
Receipt of extramural grants and contracts:					
I (faculty)	53	67	71	36	31
I (chairs)	25	62	65	44	23
S (faculty)	21	30	29	21	10
S (chairs)	17	55	42	38	13

8

What Colleagues Say about Colleagues

In this chapter, a close study is made of 108 letters of recommendation written on behalf of 108 candidates for three university positions, and of thirty-four letters of recommendation written on behalf of sixteen candidates for a college position. We begin with the assumption that such letters are written both to delineate and establish academic qualifications. We further assume that a department looking for someone to fill a vacancy would be interested in information about how an applicant might carry out his or her academic responsibilities—teaching, research, and service—and would use such letters in an effort to predict this. Surely, the letters are written with the certainty that the qualities of a candidate described are important to a reader, to members of a department seeking to recruit effective faculty. In the analysis that follows, we are most interested in what, in the assessment of academic qualifications, the letters say about a candidate's teaching.

Letters to Universities

The letters for those applying for positions at universities were written to three departments at three institutions, one in the southwest, one in the midwest, and one in the east. There are nearly equal numbers of letters for three disciplines—mathematics, psychology, and sociology. All three institutions are members of the Association of American Universities, and presumably have some research expectations for their faculty. It was anticipated that writers would understand this, and that letters would be fashioned to reflect this fact, that their contents would be representative only of what would be said about faculty seeking employment at universities.

The department chair or former chair to whom a request for the letters was made was asked to look through the files of a job search that occurred sometime after 1991 and to pull the first letter from each dossier written by a colleague or former colleague who would be in a position to evaluate a candidate's teaching. The intention was to eliminate individuals still completing their graduate work and others seeking their first full-time academic position. Here is how one chair described how he selected his sample of letters: "So I don't forget, let me record what I am doing. I open each file and try to determine if this is a new Ph.D. If so, I toss it. If not, I look for the first letter. If it is from a colleague, it goes in your pile. If it is not, I go on to the next letter.... Sometimes the first letter was clearly one that was solicited purely for teaching. Sometimes there was no mention of teaching but there was another letter entirely devoted to teaching. I included only the first letter I came across from a colleague, whether or not it addressed teaching at all."

As no attempt was made to match description with fact, what follows is perhaps as much a study of writers as of candidates. The letters are surely reflexive in that they reveal as much about the concerns, values, and perceptions of a writer as about the qualities of a candidate. To some extent, they describe the qualities writers believe readers would want to know about; there is no way of ascertaining how well any letter actually describes any candidate. The amount of attention given to teaching in a letter could reflect both how important teaching is to the writer and how important the writer believes it might be to the reader.

At the same time, since almost all of the signatures of the writers had been deleted, as were some letterheads, all that is known about the recommenders is what they might have said about themselves in a letter. Most seem to be very senior, but even this is only an impression.[1] Many were located at universities, of which only a minority were the most prestigious research centers—the University of California at Berkeley, the University of Chicago, Duke University, the Massachusetts Institute of Technology. Some letters were from colleges noted for quality undergraduate teaching—the College of William and Mary, Colorado College, Gettysburg College, Knox College.

The Place of Teaching

Given that these letters were written to research universities, the expectation that teaching would not be the main focus proved to be true.

Research was the topic generally addressed first and described in greatest detail. Information about research dominates. By far most space was devoted to it. Readers are given long and full portraits of multiple projects, results, citations, awards, and work in progress.

> Thus, the significant morbidity and mortality associated with the disease makes it an important topic of investigation. Some unique features of the disease create valuable opportunities to investigate psychological processes associated with chronic disease. Until recently, the rate of transplant rejection was approximately 35 percent. The reason for transplant failure appears to be a random event related to quality of the HLA match. [He] was able to study the effects of coping style and social support in patients both before and after a very serious negative life event (transplant rejection). Fortunately, most serious negative events occur with a relatively low frequency. From a research perspective, however, investigations of changes resulting from the random negative event are difficult. Consider the problem of investigating the effects of psychological variables on coping with negative events. First, suppose that the coping variable increases the risk of the negative event, then the two processes are inherently confounded. If the negative event occurs randomly, then the researcher can investigate the effects of personality variables independently and in interaction with the negative event. Most frequently occurring random negative events are relatively mild, and most randomly occurring serious events are relatively rare. In order to conduct a pre-to-post investigation of negative events, one either has to collect pre data on relatively mild negative events or collect very large samples for serious events. [He] realized that some of these research problems could be overcome with the…patients.

In contrast, comments about teaching are almost always brief.

> He is an excellent teacher. He treats his students with great sympathy and consideration, and he devotes truly enormous amounts of time to them.

> Overall, I would say that he strikes me as a person who is quite a dedicated teacher, that prepares meticulously his classes and that is quite worried that everybody understands him.

Sometimes the characterization of someone's teaching is even briefer. A single word—"fluent," "enthusiastic," "conscientious," "knowledgeable," "supportive," "friendly"—is all that is used in the attempt to convince a reader that a candidate is a qualified teacher. (These descriptors, of course, are also frequently used in combination with others to portray candidates.)

Academics generally profess an interest in how well others teach. Unhappy students and underenrolled classes surely do not lead to increased department budgets or size. Still, most writers here—those presumably who are as knowledgeable as anyone else about those on whose behalf they were asked to write—do not seem to know a great deal about what their colleagues do in the classroom.

Teaching occurs in a classroom or laboratory setting away from the direct observation of colleagues, administrators, and peer review committees, and these letters reflect this fact. It is a wonder that colleagues know anything about each others' teaching, and it is testimony to its importance on the part of many that some do and clumsily attempt to assess it.

In over one-fourth of these letters there is no mention of teaching or only the briefest passing comment about it, with little or no supporting evidence for the assertion ("He is a fine teacher"; "Her teaching is first class"). In the final paragraph of a two-page letter in which teaching, lecturing, or students is never alluded to, the writer concludes: "To sum up...is an effective teacher, a productive researcher, and a seasoned, skilled clinician." A second lengthy letter begins:

> Over the past several years I have had the opportunity to get to know [him] on several different levels: as a teacher, a scholar, an organizer and administrator, and a colleague. Dr.... has demonstrated a truly rare excellence in each of these areas and a perhaps rarer ability to wear all of these hats gracefully at the same time.

Again, there is no further mention of teaching until the second-to-the-last sentence: "Dr.... is an outstanding scholar and teacher; he would make a fine colleague."

Still, there are fewer letters in which there are no references to teaching than in which there are no references to collegiality or administrative work. In this sample of letters teaching comes second[2]—to be sure, often a distant second—to research. In most instances it is not an afterthought, and apologies are very rarely made for a candidate's commitment to it ("In spite of his devotion to teaching, [he] has built an enviable record of research and scholarship"). If writers do not dwell on it, it is apparently because they do not know enough about it to do so. Very seldom is it obvious that writers have little regard for teaching: "[He] will be an excellent colleague and a sympathetic teacher although, above all, his presence will significantly enhance the research profile of any department lucky enough to persuade him to join them." To be sure, such an attitude can be found throughout academia, but it would seem to be less common than critics contend.

In a not insignificant minority of letters, writers attempt to give teaching equal or more attention than research. And they can be quite specific: "He has been an exemplary teacher in this context: the depth of his thinking and the clarity of his presentations have consistently been impressive. He draws from his broad learning, which extends from philosophy and psychology to religion, history, literature, and social thought, to contextualize and extend his explications." Most often, however, it is a subject about which many have limited knowledge and they seem at sea in their efforts to praise their colleagues.

I understand that he excels in the classroom, and there is no doubt that he does.

As I mentioned earlier, I have heard him lecture [to professional audiences] on a number of occasions, and he an excellent and stimulating speaker.... I am sure he is an able teacher.

As a teacher [he] is outstanding. I base this on reports as well as the very favorable feedback I received about his teaching.... His presentations were characterized [as competent]....

The comments may sometimes be more lengthy, but they are no less vague. Many writers simply have little firsthand information about the quality of their colleagues' teaching. In fact, in a number of instances it is fairly obvious that a writer knows virtually nothing about a candidate's teaching:

Although I have not had the opportunity to observe [him] in the classroom, I have observed his performance in the role of expert consultant to our multidisciplinary research team.... I am fully confident that he would be an excellent teacher.

Overall, I would say that he strikes me as a person who is a quite dedicated teacher.

I also have the distinct impression that...is a well liked, conscientious teacher.

Writers are likely to care or know as much or more about a candidate's graduate teaching as about his or her undergraduate teaching:

I'm not sure why we leave teaching to discuss last in letters like this, but it is not because it comes last for [him]. He is an excellent teacher, both for undergraduate and graduate classes. For many years, he enthusiastically taught large lecture classes in introductory psychology, and students raved about his teaching. At the other end of the spectrum, my graduate students who have taken his neuropsychology classes can't say enough about his level of knowledge and his ability to bring the material alive with just the right historical anecdote. As a teacher, [his] first strength is in cutting-edge graduate courses and seminars. He's extremely industrious in preparation, and he sets genuinely high standards for his students. These direct teaching efforts are supplemented by a heavy investment of time in indirect supervision of both graduate and undergraduate students affiliated with his research program.

In the minds of many, merely being a successful undergraduate teacher is clearly not sufficient: "...is a very capable teacher as well as an

outstanding consultant." Someone can be described simply as a qualified researcher. On the other hand, it is not good enough to simply be a
qualified teacher. One must be something more: "He is an effective
teacher, a productive researcher, and a seasoned, skilled clinician."

Even those who could best describe a candidate's teaching after having taught one or more courses together sometimes had little to say on
the subject. This from a two-and-a-half page single-spaced letter:

> Finally, we also co-taught an undergraduate course in…. As an undergraduate
> teacher, his enthusiasm for his profession is infectious to students. He is an effec-
> tive and stimulating lecturer.

Having done research with someone seems to have more meaning
than simply having shared a classroom: "[He] and I wrote a joint paper
concerning Kurepa's hypothesis, valuated vector spaces, and abelian
groups. [He] is a bright, energetic mathematician. His mathematical
expertise as well as his research and teaching skills will be an asset to
any department. I have high regard for him as a person and as an intel-
lect. Consequently, I give him a very high recommendation."

Those who had an administrative responsibility to monitor teaching
were in the best position to know about it, and the letters reflect this.

> In my role as department chair I have visited his classroom often, and have read all
> of his course evaluations. He is a clear, articulate, engaging lecturer. The students
> love his courses, even though they are rigorous, and he consistently receives glow-
> ing evaluations. He is in high demand as an advisor as well.

> As departmental chair, I frequently hear from individual students concerning their
> reactions to their professors. This is not always fun. When the professor is…however,
> the comments have without exception been very favorable…. He has taught intro-
> ductory linear algebra, ordinary differential equations, and complex analysis. My
> evaluation of his work in these courses is based on personal observation in one class,
> student evaluation forms, unsolicited comments from students, and reports from other
> faculty…. I observed [him] teach a class in linear algebra, in which he discussed
> orthonormal bases and the Gram-Schmidt process. I was impressed with several things
> about the class. His response to questions about the previous homework assignment
> were straightforward and lucid. His explanation of the new material was clear, and
> accompanied by very helpful geometry on the blackboard, rendered exceptionally
> neatly. He frequently asked for questions, and responded to them in a way that indi-
> cated to me that he understood what was troubling the student, and was able to pro-
> vide just the clarification the student needed. He clearly held the attention of the
> class. The atmosphere was one of cordiality and mutual respect.

Instances in which teaching is discussed in such detail were rare, a bit surprisingly, less so for mathematicians than for psychologists or sociologists.

The most solid evidence a writer had to support the assessment of a candidate's teaching after the out-of-the-ordinary classroom visit was indirect, namely, student evaluation, formal and informal. Here is the gist of student responses to five mathematicians, all of whom coincidentally seem to be among the best teachers in their departments:

> He taught several calculus courses and a vector analysis course. I read some of his teaching evaluations and they contained many positive comments such as "excellent teacher"; "he taught the subject of math well and showed enthusiasm in the classroom"; "very impressed with [him], well prepared and stimulating." His teaching evaluations ranked him among the better teachers of the department.

> I also learned from these comments that he is extremely helpful to individual students outside the classroom. I might add that [his] student evaluations in calculus are among the best in the department. As one calculus student wrote: "Professor...was the finest math professor I've met and probably will ever meet."

> He taught two precalculus classes for business students and received outstanding ratings from the students (probably the highest for any first year class). He takes teaching very seriously and does a wonderful job.

> On his teaching evaluations he was rated between a 3.9 and 4.1 on a scale of 1-5. Here are a few exact quotes from student evaluations of [him]: "The instructor is great;" "Great teacher. Well organized and always willing to answer questions;" "He's funny at times and competent—I always come to the lecture even though it's not required which is rare for me;" "Excellent instructor—knows his stuff;" "[He] is very good at interacting with the students;" "He was very good, very easy to understand."

> He took great pains with his more advanced courses as well: for instance, his topology students wrote: "He enjoys the subject intensely, that is necessary and sufficient"; "He is a disciplined professor with the ability to deal with all students and he is always well-prepared when it comes to the subject matter"; "Prof.... is an asset to the math department, I hate to know that he will be leaving next year."

Rather than overlook teaching, there is an obvious attempt to portray candidates as shining in the classroom. If anything, writers might be overselling candidate's pedagogical skills; there seems to be no average teachers, but then with grade inflation there also no longer seems to be average students.

The clearest sign that teaching is not taken with the greatest seriousness is not that it is ignored, but that in the letters candidates are nearly always described as "excellent," "superb," "first-rate," "superior," "the best," "gifted," and the like. Almost everyone is an outstanding teacher. In only two of the 108 letters is a candidate described as less than satisfactory in the classroom.

> However, in his teaching to the unmotivated and mathematically unprepared student he appears to have even more of a struggle than the rest of us.
>
> I must say that during the years he was here, his lecturing left something to be desired. He received public speaking instruction, with what effect I do not know.

In light of all of this, it would seem that everyone has great teaching ability, that writers do not know enough about this quality of those about whom they write to make a careful evaluation, or that writers do not care enough about the subject to attempt to make a balanced assessment. In light of the fact that so much of it is based on hearsay, in the end, all of the praise is not terribly convincing.

The Place of Students

How a faculty member relates to students is a matter given a great deal of attention in a number of letters. A central point of the testimony of many writers is that a candidate truly cares about students. It is sometimes as important to show that someone is as nurturant as competent. One can be "demanding," "rigorous," or have "high standards" as long as he or she is "generous with time" or "sympathetic." Being available to students and being helpful are crucial.

> He goes as much the extra mile with the "service" students as he does with the mathematics majors.
>
> They were impressed with his enthusiasm for teaching and his willingness to help them outside of class. [He was] eager to help.
>
> I have also noticed that he is consistently helpful and patient during his office hours. His students clearly find him approachable, and they visit him frequently in his office.

Knowing how to relate to students is a distinct asset. Sympathy, compassion, tolerance, and being accommodating are often highlighted. The letters indicate that serving students is viewed as part of an academic's responsibility, not something to be avoided or for which one risks being punished. The ultimate measure of being a successful teacher is relating well to students.

> [He] is also a caring and inspiring teacher of boundless energy. Students are often enthralled with his animated lectures and personable style. It is common to see [him] surrounded by students after class or in his office talking with him, debating, laughing, or just plain "hanging out."

I was also impressed with...willingness to take every comment seriously.... All this resulted in very stimulating class sessions with a highly interactive group of students.

He seems to develop an easy rapport with his students; they readily respond to open-ended questions in class, seek him out after class, and are respectful and attentive in his presence. Perhaps the most impressive aspect of his teaching was his ability and willingness to organize a volunteer experience for his students.

In the end, it would seem, teaching is of some importance. If it were not, the professoriate would surely give less consideration to how students feel about their instruction and instructors.

And I know that he is held in high regard.... His teaching style is characterized by enthusiasm and good humor. His lectures do more than inform, they inspire.

He is entertaining and instructive. The students love him.

She is also a fabulous teacher, the type of devoted and committed professor who leaves lasting impressions on students in terms of their critical consciousness and the direction of their lives.... I have no doubt she would soon be one of the most popular teachers in your department.

Serving students is clearly part of academic culture. What some fail to understand is that it might not be the dominant value for some of the professoriate—particularly those who teach at universities—some or all of the time.

It is obvious that faculty consider it their responsibility to serve students. As chapter 10 will make quite clear, even university faculty do a great deal more for students than academic administrators.

Letters to a College

The college from which the letters were obtained had advertised that it had an opening in its department of history and government for someone with experience teaching political science. In its catalogue, it is described as a "a private, non-sectarian, co-educational, career-oriented liberal arts college." It was also noted that the college "places primary emphasis on excellence in teaching and learning." The institution has between eighty and 100 full-time faculty, and the department of history and government has a faculty of four, three of whom had earned Ph.D.s.

The quality of a candidate's teaching and a commitment to students are given considerable weight in twenty-seven of the thirty-four letters to the college. (Five of the seven writers, who almost ignore the matter

of teaching, hold appointments at research universities.) The majority
of letters begin with a discussion of the candidates' teaching—at least,
what they have taught, what they can teach, and their qualifications as
teachers. Few do not go directly to the subject of teaching:

> The credentials he submits independently will establish his background for the
> particular appointment. My own purpose in writing is to assure the members of the
> search committee that they and their students are certain to be very pleased with
> [his] performance.

> [He] is a most capable and caring professor. He makes students think and
> reflect...in a personal way.

> She is a great favorite with the students, and her willingness to spend time with
> them and to supervise their independent studies is unusual even at [this very pres-
> tigious New England teaching institution].

> I know that many letters of recommendation indicate that an applicant is an excel-
> lent teacher. However, in the case of Mr.... I cannot emphasize this point too
> much. His teaching ability far surpasses most instructors. The reason he is such an
> excellent instructor is that he simply enjoys teaching. He can communicate his
> enjoyment of the subject and students typically respond to that quality in a highly
> positive fashion. I guess the jargon I should use is that he has the ability to be
> interactive. [He] invites participation on the part of his students and he is adept at
> massaging it out of them when they refuse the invitation. His student
> evaluations...certainly indicate that [he] is a superior teacher.... Basically, [stu-
> dent evaluations] indicate that his lecture style is extremely effective. His presenta-
> tions of the material are interesting and keep the students' attention. They state that
> he has the ability to relate well with the students, and he has a good sense of humor.
> Finally, they say that although he has his own point of view on various issues, he is
> very good about covering all different opinions.

At least one letter for all but one of the candidates describes him or
her as "one of the finest" or in such superlative terms (e.g., "outstanding;" "one of the most popular;" "a great teacher"). A number of writers
are obviously convinced that the individual they are recommending is
without peers ("an electrifying classroom presence;" "charismatic in
teaching") as a teacher, and that they cannot say enough about the impact he or she will have on students. It is a wonder that—with so many
faculty who apparently love to teach, who are dedicated and committed
to undergraduates, who are enthusiastic, conscientious, and patient, who
have great rapport in small or large classes, who generate enthusiasm,
curiosity, and above all, confidence—there is such widespread criticism
about undergraduate teaching and there is so little evidence around the
country of student learning, a chronic faculty complaint.

Many writers have little direct knowledge about the teaching of the candidate they are recommending, and they are general and vague: "By all reports..."; "She is articulate and has a wide intellectual reach, qualities that are important for a good teacher"; "I understand..."; "Although I haven't directly observed...in the classroom, we have shared some students." It is widely believed that communication skills and teaching skills are the same thing.

On the other hand, others, having visited candidates' classrooms or even having co-taught with them, can be quite specific: "I personally had the pleasure of observing four of his classes, and found him to have a strong talent for Socratic interaction and for integrating the anecdotal into broad conceptual frameworks. He consistently maintained realistically high standards for student performance, and served as a role model for those standards by virtue of his conscientious and extensive lecture preparations." In addition, some writers reviewed course syllabi, while others analyzed and compared student evaluations. A few based their conclusions on trends in course enrollments.

Other Qualities

After the subject of teaching, the letters give most attention to candidates' personalities and those characteristics that might make individuals desirable colleagues. The traits apparently thought to be most attractive are, alphabetically: cheerfulness ("a sunny disposition"; "positive"), cooperativeness ("a team player"), decency ("a gentleman"; "treats colleagues with consideration, respect, fairness, and kindness"), dependability ("never failed us"), hard working or energetic, helpfulness, outgoing, pleasantness (courteous; "likeable to students, staff, and faculty"; "always affable"), relaxed, reliability, a (great) sense of humor ("funny and refreshing"), stable (balanced; consistent; mature; "sobriety of character"), stimulating ("he has flair"), straightforward, and unselfishness.

There would seem to be a premium on colleagues who are friendly and personable, who are nonthreatening and supportive, who possess "good spirit" and are "always willing to serve students and the college." The majority of writers see the academic world as a place where people want to be liked and want to like their colleagues. They want colleagues who "fit in...personally and professionally."

A number, but a far smaller proportion of letters, also mention the quality of a candidate's training, the quality of scholarship, and the quality of someone's mind. References are also made to a range of experiences ("he has traveled widely") or interests ("he can teach courses in several areas"; "he has taught an array of social science courses"; "he has taught political science, geography, business ethics, and economics"), research interests, academic accomplishments ("[the] second book will be reissued this fall and I expect it to receive favorable reviews"), and administrative capacities. Some of these matters are occasionally discussed at length, given as much attention as teaching. A number of writers obviously want to avoid leaving the impression that a candidate is a narrow specialist who would not be able and willing to prepare an array of new courses on a regular bases. Finally, a candidate's religious practices are sometimes mentioned: "Dr.... is a very active member of our church. He teaches Sunday school and volunteers his time to participate in other activities." It was unclear whether this was done to reflect morality or conventionality.

Some letters close with a statement that ties teaching to scholarship, referring to teaching and research accomplishments (or potential). In sum, other matters are clearly not ignored, but not surprisingly they are of secondary concern compared to teaching: "As a teacher and colleague [here, he] was energetic and innovative. I recall in particular his interest in designing new courses, lecture series, etc. that would be of interest and help to the students. His teaching was also first-rate. The scope of his education is so broad that he was able to put life into the most mundane topics." Such individuals—even if "demanding, but fair"—are "cherished" by student and other college faculty.

Notes

1. In actuality, more is known about the candidates, as their research and experience are sometimes discussed in some detail. We could also readily determine that of the 108, eighteen (two mathematicians, six psychologists, and ten sociologists) were female.
2. Besides research and teaching, being able to get along with others is a subject that receives notable attention in these letters, particularly those for females:

   [She] also is a superb colleague. She always pulls her load and more, has exceptional social skills, and is a fountain of good sense. Her social skills are truly exceptional, and they facilitate not only her dealings with students and colleagues, but also the functioning of departmental activities. It would be hard to imagine our department without [her].

On a personal level [she] is a delightful person to have in the department. She is totally straightforward and cooperative in departmental affairs. She will fit in well into any situation.

Finally, [she] would be a wonderful colleague to have in any department. She is a generous and open person, interested and interesting, who also happens to have a fantastic sense of humor.

9

The Academic Labor Market in Action

It is apparent from the materials reviewed in chapter 2 that not only is there not an all-encompassing academic labor market, but there is not a single labor market for any one academic discipline. There is a distinct labor market in every discipline for those whose academic work involves research in addition to teaching; the labor market for those who teach and do not do research is more inchoate. Colleges interested in hiring faculty to instruct undergraduates certainly advertise formally and sometimes go to great lengths to find someone to meet their needs. However, for the most part they present these needs in quite general terms. Indeed, they are often very vague. An English department at a college may need two or three literature courses taught; it frequently is not important which ones from a list of five or six these are. The survey course on the nineteenth-century novel can be scheduled for next year; this semester, Shakespearean drama can be offered. Moreover, it is commonly assumed that anyone with an advanced degree in the field can teach just about any undergraduate course a department needs to offer.

Openings for Teachers

It is incontrovertible that the majority of openings for teachers in any discipline are so broadly defined that the needs of the buyer and the skills of the seller may not be effectually matched. Buyers are nonspecific about their needs; they cast very wide nets. Sellers, who want jobs and who want to please, can be quite adaptable in presenting their interests and qualifications. This is facilitated by the fact that their reputations are strictly local. Thus, as buyers do not define their needs in such a way as to find the most skillful candidates, and as sellers can suggest that they are something they are not, the academic labor market for teachers is, at most, nominal. Buyers often do not have a very good idea of what they are getting; sellers may be unsure of what is being purchased.

A rational pairing of a buyer and a seller may not even be a primary concern in filling a position. An institution may be clear about some of the qualities it would like prospective candidates to have—most often, experience, enthusiasm, and a desire to excel in the classroom: "A proven commitment to excellence in teaching is mandatory"; "We would like someone with excellent teaching ability or potential"; "True instructional excellence and interest are of the highest priority." It is less likely to designate the expertise it would like applicants to have. Colleges seem most determined to find someone with the requisite degree. Beyond that, they are not always sure what they want individuals to know or teach.

Fewer openings for college teachers are announced in disciplinary or professional publications than in publications with a more general readership, such as urban newspapers or the *Chronicle of Higher Education.* This is most true for the sciences. Some positions for those who teach and do research are only in disciplinary or professional publications. These points are well exemplified in how vacancies are advertised and filled for a graduate department of chemistry, which is discussed in some detail later in this chapter.

We begin with an examination of 450 advertisements published in three different sources between 1991 and 1994 for teachers of chemistry at institutions of higher learning—many specifying that their programs were accredited by the American Chemical Society. For the most part, these advertisements indicate that there is less interest in competence or disciplinary specialization than in personal characteristics that would make someone attractive to students and colleagues: "Candidates should be...compatible with our missions and goals...[and] have an interest in becoming fully involved in campus life"; "The ability to interact successfully with students is necessary."

Not surprisingly, teaching is mentioned first or early in all but a handful of these advertisements. Advising freshmen and departmental majors was indicated considerably less often. "The ability to communicate" was also a *sine qua non* for many positions. Taking the full context of the advertisement into account, the meaning of this was often vague. What subarea of chemistry a successful candidate might be expected to teach was also sometimes unclear. Buyers wanted organic chemists who would be willing or able to teach biochemistry, physical chemists with analytical teaching experience, general chemists who could on occasion teach biology, organic or inorganic chemists able to teach physical chemistry. Much of the time it apparently is more important to have an individual who teach a variety of courses, some even interdisciplinary, than someone with clearly demarcated professional or research interests. There is absolutely no question that institutions are looking for teachers, not scientists.

> Chemistry: Clayton State College, serving south metropolitan Atlanta, invites applications for an academic-year, tenure-track position in chemistry effective September, 1993. Rank and salary negotiable depending upon qualifications. Doctorate in chemistry required. Teaching experience and a commitment to effective student learning are expected; ability to teach critical thinking course helpful. Primary responsibilities will be teaching general-education and program-specific courses in chemistry; serving on faculty committees and working actively with other faculty in the ongoing development of the general education program; advising students and assisting with their registration into classes; engaging in continuing growth as a professional; supporting the goals of the college, and performing other duties...assigned.

> Chemistry: Analytical/inorganic/physical. Applicants are sought with expertise in one or more of these areas to teach undergraduate general chemistry, physical or analytical (alternate years) and occasionally non-major chemistry beginning August 21, 1991. Ph.D. and teaching experience required, background in instrumentation...and computers preferred. Rank and salary dependent upon qualifications. Undergraduate research encouraged but not required. Jamestown College is a four-year liberal arts institution affiliated with the Presbyterian Church and seeks a person with a commitment to non-sectarian Christian higher education.

As far as many buyers are concerned, those who teach need a great deal more—most obviously, "a personality that will appeal to undergraduates"—than mastery of a discipline.

Colleges expected candidates who would contribute to the teaching program, who had been successful teachers, who could articulate their interest in teaching undergraduates, who could mentor undergraduates, who were able to interact with students, who wanted to become involved in active learning and teaching, and who had developed unique teaching techniques. As suggested, a candidate who might be evaluated favorably by students while teaching them a little less chemistry would be as desirable as a candidate capable of teaching more chemistry but who lacked social skills valued by students, and even colleagues. (A number of advertisements reminded applicants: "Send student evaluations.")

Candidates were four times as likely to be asked to provide information relating to their teaching—their interest, their conception, or their philosophy—than to their research: "Candidates should address their views about teaching (rather than research)"; "Candidates should include a statement of their philosophy of Christian higher education."

Most often when an advertisement specified research it was to indicate that a candidate's research program should be oriented to working with undergraduates: "Student-faculty research encouraged"; "Must be able to develop a research program which involves undergraduates"; "Student participation in research is necessary"; "Must be willing to sponsor undergraduate research." Candidates had to know what sort of tasks would be appropriate for undergraduates, and how to supervise them. Collaborative research with undergraduates is what colleges want, not faculty preoccupied with their own research. More than one announcement for a "full-time renewable" or "tenure-track" position stated "research not required." A majority of the time a principal responsibility in such cases was "directing undergraduate student research."

> Chemistry: Creighton University invites applications for the position of assistant professor in organic chemistry, to begin in the fall of 1993. This is an entry-level, tenure-track position. A Ph.D. and evidence of potential for excellent teaching and research at the undergraduate level are required. The successful candidate will be expected to share the teaching of the organic chemistry and non-major courses and to develop an active research program involving undergraduates.

> Chemistry: Grinnell College invites applications for a tenure-track appointment as assistant professor (associate professor possible) of chemistry, beginning in August, 1993. The appointee will be expected to teach organic chemistry, to contribute to the teaching of introductory and general education courses, and to develop a research program that involves undergraduate students. A Ph.D. in chemistry is required, and a strong interest in teaching in an undergraduate liberal-arts environment that emphasizes close faculty-student interaction is expected.

Clearly, colleges in the market for chemistry teachers are not necessarily looking for the most qualified or creative chemists. Nor do they always want someone who could teach the most about chemistry; they do not need that. They, first of all, need students. They also need students who are not disgruntled, who are convinced that their lack of success is their own fault and has little to do with the competence of their instructors. They are determined to find individuals with qualities that would be most adaptable to the institution's culture.

Generally, precepts that exert influence on other labor markets are mostly imperceptible here. The labor market for those who teach and do research is markedly different. The fact that a distinct labor market exists for such appointments is by itself noteworthy.

Openings for Teachers/Researchers

Of course, the expectations for faculty being recruited to teach and do research are quite different from those who are expected only to teach. Buyers are interested in a great deal more than a commitment to teaching and the institution. Teaching is as a matter of form alluded to in almost all of the advertisements, but largely to describe the overall responsibilities of a position, simply to note that teaching is part of the job: "Teaching involves..."; "The successful candidate will be expected to teach..."; "Must be qualified to teach..."; "Duties will include...." At the same time, a number of advertisements do specify that applicants must be "effective" teachers.

It is pretty well taken for granted that candidates will have had postdoctoral research experience: "Postdoctoral experience is expected"; "Postdoctoral experience preferred." Without question, postdoctoral experience is more highly valued than teaching experience. It is also taken for granted that candidates have a clearly defined specialization in chemistry. And it is taken for granted that candidates not only have a well-developed research agenda in mind, but want single-mindedly to pursue it: "We are seeking a Ph.D. who will establish a vigorous research program in any area of theoretical chemistry"; "To develop an active, funded research program."

As buyers see it, one aspect of the dedication to research is skill in obtaining grants: "The successful candidate...will be expected to aggressively pursue outside funding"; "[To] conduct a nationally-competitive, funded research program"; "develop a productive, externally-funded research program." Some advertisements specify that applicants have the capability to write grant proposals. As one advertisement put it: "The department has a tradition of substantial extramural research funding."

In most cases, departments pay at least lip service to the teaching dimension, but not always.

Louisiana State University invites applications for a tenure-track assistant professor position for persons with research interests in physical, organic or biophysical chemistry, including, but not limited to, the following areas: molecular recognition, organized media, supramolecular chemistry, or drug design. Teaching responsibilities will be in organic chemistry. Ph.D. in chemistry with postdoctoral or equivalent related experience required. The department has twenty-seven research-active faculty that attract research funding of ca. $4 M per year. It has outstanding analytical and computing facilities and also has excellent opportunities at LSU's synchrotron light source.

The Department of Chemistry of the University of Chicago invites applications from outstanding individuals for the position of assistant professor. Applications from people with interest in any area of physical chemistry will be considered. Postdoctoral experience is preferred. Applicants should submit a curriculum vitae, a list of publications, and a succinct outline of their research plans. Candidates should arrange for three letters of recommendation to be sent directly....

Assistant professor of chemistry, Rice University. (Tenure-track) Imaginative and energetic candidates are sought in areas of experimental physical chemistry which complement Rice University's initiative in nanoscience and nanotechnology. Emphasis will be placed on innovative research programs which transcend traditional boundaries, especially those concerned with the study of matter on a nanometer scale. Candidates should send letters of recommendation, a resume, and a description of their proposed research to....

Institutions seeking those who teach and do research definitely do not want generalists, but specialists. The capitalized first words for some advertisements are the research skills a department is looking for: "NMR SPECTROSCOPIST/ASSISTANT PROFESSOR"; "FACULTY POSITION: MASS SPECTROMETRY." Lists of publications, reprints, and a statement of research interests are asked for more frequently than particulars about teaching: "A concise statement of research interests is necessary"; "Include a succinct summary of research"; "Applicants should submit a statement of research plans and objectives"; "Submit... a one- or two-page summary of research plans accompanied by more detailed proposals." In short, buyers are most interested in evidence that bears on how productive as a scientist an applicant will be. They expect "substantial" indications of "outstanding accomplishments" or "motivation toward excellence in research." These documents unambiguously indicate that other matters are secondary.

The Labor Market for Those Who Teach and Do Research

It is possible to get a fairly accurate picture of how the academic labor market works by looking closely at how research universities and colleges recruit faculty for positions that involve both teaching and research.

For an example of the former, a number of particulars about two job searches by a chemistry department of a large public university were therefore collected. One search was for an organic chemist and the other was for an analytical chemist. (Hereafter, one will be referred to as search x and the other as search y.) One opening was for an assistant professor, while the other was at the senior level, for an associate or full professor. Both were conducted in the 1990s.

The department offers a Ph.D., and is ranked somewhere in the top forty to sixty of the close to 150 departments that grant about 95 percent of the Ph.D.s awarded in chemistry by American universities. It is a fairly typical graduate department in that its faculty of around two dozen conduct research primarily in the four traditional areas of chemistry—analytical, inorganic, organic, and physical. It has nearly 125 graduate students and supports two dozen postdoctoral associates. Substantial research grants support the work of two-thirds of the faculty.

For both searches, advertisements were placed in the *Chemical and Engineering News,* the major disciplinary source for such announcements, and also in *Science* for search y. For each search, between 250 and 275 solicitations were sent to chairs of chemistry departments listed in the "Directory of Graduate Research," and another fifty to eighty letters went to leading scientists in each specialty at major research centers who might be able to identify suitable candidates. In both cases, over three dozen prospective candidates, especially members of minority or protected groups, were also contacted and invited to apply. There were eighty-eight applicants for one position, and 116 for the other. A pool of the most qualified candidates was identified by a departmental subcommittee of specialists in each area, and from this a short list of individuals to invite for an interview was developed.

The department was most interested in the candidates' job experience; a listing of publications (for evidence of both a relatively high and consistent rate and independent work), particularly papers in major journals (e.g., *Journal of the American Chemical Society*); record of major research grants ("His record of research support is outstanding both from non-federal and federal sources"; "Characteristic of his successful start ...is externally funded through NIH at a time when such funding is exceptionally tough to come by"); visibility in the field; and teaching experience and effectiveness—applications were to include "a statement of teaching goals and interests."

For both searches, the department placed a high priority on finding someone whose research program would complement those of other members of the department. Postdoctoral research experience—where, with whom, and how it related to a candidate's development as a scientist—was an explicit (at least, "highly recommended") prerequisite for the junior position. The department was looking for evidence of an applicant's ability: "(a) to initiate and develop an independent research program; (b) to obtain research funding; (c) to manage and educate Ph.D.-level graduate students; (d) to teach effectively at the undergraduate and graduate levels in areas complementary to those of the present …faculty; and (e) to cooperate and work within and external to the Department of Chemistry."

In gathering information, the department relied primarily on submitted resumes, telephone calls to and from friends and prestigious scientists, and letters of recommendation—from previous and current research advisors, scientific collaborators, and others familiar with "the applicant's professional abilities."

Although many times written by friends of a candidate and full of generalities and hyperbole, the letters were given considerable weight. Twelve letters of recommendation were found in the file of one candidate. Not surprisingly, for a number of candidates, some writers disagreed with others in their assessments of promise, ability, quality of research, rate of productivity, and leadership potential [(1) "However, he will need at least one additional major grant in order to expand his program to attain national recognition," versus "He is becoming recognized as one of the top chemists of his generation," versus "He is on the verge of attaining international stature in his field"; (2) "Although he has not been enormously productive as measured by his publication record.…" versus "His scientific production is significant, original, and abundant," versus "While it is true he has amassed only a modest publication list.…"]. There were enough assertions in the many letters collected for any candidate for readers to draw almost any portrait they wished.

There was much less information gathered about a candidate's teaching. Most of what was said was favorable, although somewhat circumstantial. When provided, comments by students were very favorable (of course, it is unlikely that a candidate would submit negative critiques), but again sometimes contradictory: "[He] was very effective and thorough in all his lectures. I think the only problem is that it was paced too fast," versus "Excellent lecturer. Slow but not too slow at explaining the material," versus "He seems to go over the material a little too fast."

According to the department chair, selecting the most promising applicants was straightforward and a relatively easy matter:

> The evaluation of the ranking of the top candidates proceeded by evaluating the research proposals as evidence of independent, creative research design and statements on teaching and the result of lectures given during the interview, to assess teaching ability. A primary goal of evaluating the candidates is the assessment of whether the proposed research is creative and novel, would attract external funding, and is sufficiently independent...to provide a clear record of originality on the part of the candidate.... Senior...faculty have...served as program managers at NSF...and...especially has a long record of experience in judging the quality and content of research.

There were a number of reasons why some candidates were not deemed suitable to interview or judged not to be sufficiently qualified for the position. Nothing more aptly reflects faculty values than the numerous following examples of comments:

> "AA did not qualify for the short-list of candidates interviewed because AA's research productivity was judged to be substantially below those of our finalist. In particular, AA has averaged less than one research publication/year during...fourteen years as an independent investigator. These are solid publications, but not of sufficiently high quality to change the negative impression created by the low overall output."

> "(1) [His] publication record is demonstrably weaker than that of...(the number one finalist), but is comparable to that of the other finalists. (2) Questions were raised about BB's potential to continue to obtain funding for his research program because of the incompatibility of his research objectives with those of the major funding agencies. (3) [He] was judged by some to be quiet, reclusive, and unlikely to develop strong interactions."

> "However, much of his research is in areas peripheral to...chemistry and few of his publications are in journals familiar to...chemists."

> "Furthermore, he was unable to provide sufficient evidence of the ability to run an independent research program at a major university. Thus, while he is listed as co-investigator on several research grants, he has rarely served as the principal investigator."

> "CC's record of research as an independent investigator was inadequate to justify consideration for a tenured position."

> "DD was not able to provide sufficient evidence of the ability to develop an independent program of research in this country."

"The lack of substantively innovative ideas in EE's research plans, and the concern over future funding possibilities are the major reasons [that he was not ranked higher]."

"In addition, there is a significant overlap in FF's research and that of other faculty members in the department."

"GG's research plan was not well described. GG's presentation of... research...proposals during the interview led to the discovery of a flaw in GG's understanding of the mechanisms underlying...formation processes GG proposed to study.... [I]t was clear that GG would have to make major changes in the research plan.... However, that and the fact that GG's projects were not at the same level of sophistication as HH's in a similar area were the basis to not consider making an offer."

"This is likely because II's postdoctoral experience has not resulted in much original research; II has been taken up with constructing new instruments."

"This research area is sufficiently different from JJ's Ph.D. studies to make JJ attractive in both...but has not come to full fruition yet."

"KK's main shortcoming was in his research proposal. It is a direct extension of his current postdoctoral research.... [T]he faculty were concerned about the lack of new directions and ideas in his research plans, and the lack of a clear break from his postdoctoral mentor."

"Also, it is hard to know how competitive LL's research will be in...the area he will compete in."

"The chemistry faculty felt he was a strong candidate, but with far less experience and sophistication in his research plan than the top ranked candidate."

"MM does not have postdoctoral experience."

"NN had research interests in...directly overlapping with Professor...."

"[His] plans for research were a direct continuation of his postdoctoral efforts, and concerns about the discrimination between his postdoctoral mentor's research program and his future independent research were the factors which placed him below...in the evaluation."

Those candidates invited for an interview were expected to give a formal presentation dealing with their research. During the visit, they met individually with faculty in their specialty area, with members of the department personnel committee, with the department chair, with the dean, and, on occasion, with other faculty. Interested faculty were asked to complete a form evaluating candidates (the categories were: "wonderful," "satisfactory," "marginal," or "mediocre") on six dimensions: understanding of research field, formal presentation, suitability for department, intelligence, drive, and maturity. A general assessment was asked for: "a hot prospect, sure to succeed," "will probably do well, good choice," "ambivalent," or "do not make offer." There was also a section for general comments:

"I would think...would be a top line addition. He's got all the right characteristics. I support him for FULL PROF."

"Not prepared with regard to start-up funds. At this point his requests would seem to be modest. A...chemist with...leanings looks good. He would like to achieve a 'small' group of [about] ten-twelve."

"I found little chemistry in...seminar. It isn't clear to me how much chemical sense, versus instrumental sense...has."

[For the candidate above] "I'm convinced that this is the right person for us, for...chemistry...breadth of interests."

Not unexpectedly, there were no explicit remarks on these sheets on aspects of the candidates' presentations that might relate to teaching.

The final rankings of the candidates for both searches were made by the faculty in the respective areas and were presented to the entire faculty for a vote: "At the personnel committee meeting today, the results of the open search x were considered. The order suggested by the [specialty] division...was accepted unanimously. Offering...a position as professor of chemistry was also approved unanimously. Should [he] decline our offer, an offer of a position as professor of chemistry for... was approved by the personnel committee by a vote of three for, zero against, and one abstain."

The evidence is overwhelming that candidates were largely evaluated and selected here according to a single criterion, research—what they have done and what they might do. Quite simply, the controlling concern was whether they would bring money and visibility to the department. There were random comments about teaching—essentially always positive—but these were given little notice. One semifinalist submitted a nineteen-page research plan and no record could be found about his experience or views on teaching. To be sure, the expectation of good teaching was ritually mentioned; there was no indication, however, that anyone in the hiring department paid much attention to the subject. The most benign interpretation that could be given to the noted absence of concern with regard to teaching was that all of the candidates impressed their hosts as equally able teachers.

The chair's assessment of the candidate eventually offered one of the positions summarizes pretty well the views of his colleagues: "[He was] the unanimous choice for the top candidate. [He] demonstrated a far superior ability to construct a new and unique research program which was not derivative of his previous postdoctoral experience.... However, because of [his] dual postdoctoral experiences, his maturity in developing an independent research program made a more clear and definitive demonstration."

These data leave little doubt that teaching is at best marginal in the academic labor market for individuals expected to teach and do research. The fact is less surprising than the indignation, posturing, and denial— and public proclamations—it effects.

The Search for a College Teacher

In contrast, when a college is in need of a faculty member, the matter of teaching is, as the first section of this chapter made evident, highlighted. On the face of it, it would, of course, be expected that other considerations would pretty much diminish in importance; and in large part most do. Scholarly and scientific ability clearly fade into the background. As suggested, often the fact that someone has the requisite degree is adequate evidence of disciplinary competence. At the same time, other factors that are at best only marginally related to how individuals present themselves to students become more salient. Since the amount of reliable information about someone's teaching that can be collected is relatively small, and since the faculty and administration of a college have concerns that transcend the teaching of students, these other factors often become critical in determining who in the end is selected for a position.

In the search for a college teacher, it would be stretching the meaning of the term to conclude that the labor market operates to match buyers and sellers. By way of example, we can look at a search by a division of liberal arts of a college for a faculty member to teach English.

In its catalogue, the college describes itself as "an independent, urban, coeducational institution...[that] provides liberal arts and professional programs for more than 1800 graduate and undergraduate students in day, evening, week-end, and summer sessions." It was founded by an order of nuns after the turn of the century as the first college for women in the area, and became coeducational in the early 1970s. Besides English, the faculty in the division of liberal arts have degrees in and teach economics, foreign languages, history, philosophy, political science, psychology, and sociology.

In response to an advertisement published in the *Chronicle of Higher Education,* 139 individuals applied for the position. For the use of his colleagues on the search committee, one of the members ranked all of the candidates on five criteria: whether or not they had a Ph.D., the quality (or prestige) of the institution where they earned their degree, whether they had teaching experience, the breadth of their interest, and whether they had any publications.

It was difficult to determine how effective candidates would be as teachers, as almost all were described in letters of recommendation by terms such as "excellent," "superior," "the best," and the like.

> She is patient, organized, thorough, receptive to student input, and respectful of students and ideas. Over the years, many students who have taken courses from her have spoken to me about her outstanding teaching.

> The quality of...teaching has been superb [here], whether in the freshman composition course or in the upper division literature course. Teaching evaluations are always among the highest in the department, results that are consistent with glowing reports from faculty observers.

> His reputation as a teacher [here] is very high indeed.

> He is an unusually good teacher.... His student teaching evaluations here are consistently in the very top range.

Here is yet another sample of letters in which the vocabulary of merit is degraded through hyperbole.

Candidates also go to great lengths to present themselves as committed teachers, with a deep and ever-abiding passion for pedagogy:

> I believe in the importance of a student-centered approach to teaching.... I am committed to expanding my skills in an ongoing effort to teach as effectively as I can. I am eager to extend the teaching abilities I have developed in these courses to work with students in introductory and advanced courses in literature as well as composition.... Teaching in an undergraduate-focused environment has long been my goal. As a student at...I developed a desire to teach at a similar institution and to offer my students the same commitment to teaching that I enjoyed in my professors. This desire was strengthened during my participation in a mentorship program.

> My teaching methods all have a common goal: to actively involve each and every student in the class. To this end, I have developed various methods that encourage close reading and foster lively classroom discussion.... I anticipate a career in which I teach composition and literature through an interdisciplinary approach, develop courses which focus on literature and the environment, [etc].

> I enjoy teaching composition very much, in part because it raises my own awareness about the conventions of writing.

Candidates clearly know that they will not be teaching highly specialized courses; they are letting the college know that they are aware of this fact and that they will be dedicated teachers who will care about and nurture students. Some even submitted course syllabi—never for advanced courses—and other evidence of their teaching skills with their credentials. (Actually, more submitted samples of their writing.) If nothing else, the youthful optimism and enthusiasm on the part of so many is certainly touching.

The committee members charged with finding the most appropriate candidates spent many hours paring the list. Unfortunately, in about 80 percent of the cases, on strictly academic criteria, there was not much to distinguish one candidate from another. On paper, most appeared suitable; just about anyone could be expected to do at least an adequate job.

Committee members prepared lists and shared these with their colleagues. To call the attention of other committee members to a particular candidate, simple labels were often applied: "been away," "Berkeley," "black," "fishy," "friends in high places," "ideologue," "lesbian," "local," "Mormon," "odd," "theoretical," "weird." In some cases, it was not entirely clear whether the intent of a label was to further an applicant's candidacy or to undercut it. A single phrase, for example, "quite eager to please" or "very cool" might be seen by some as a compliment, but by others as pejorative.

In their deliberations, the question of someone's teaching was never far from most committee members' minds. For twelve of the sixteen applicants who made the first two cuts, the question of teaching was scrutinized most closely: "wide range of teaching"; "teaching seems solid"; "pushes himself as teacher"; "teaching is the question."

Yet, besides the letters of recommendation and the crafted statements by the candidates regarding their devotion and success as teachers, there was no way of knowing who would best serve students. The committee members did know, however, who would make them comfortable— whom faculty could work with, who would not be a disruptive force, who would most easily fit in—and ultimately these concerns apparently were controlling. In the end, the committee members selected someone who at various times had taught for the college, someone who was as qualified as any other applicant, but someone whom they knew, trusted, and liked—whom they could work with, who would not be a disruptive force, who would fit in, who would be affable.

Obviously, colleges do take chances. They do not always hire local candidates. They do hire outsiders, relative strangers, those about whom they know relatively little. It cannot even be concluded from a single case that local candidates are routinely given special preference. Clearly, they sometimes are, and this is one instance of that fact. One example surely is not evidence that the academic labor market for college teachers is completely nonexistent. Nonetheless, it does suggest that, to the degree that it does operate, the market can be somewhat irrelevant in spite of outward appearances; it is not always the case that after a national pool of candidates is generated, a local candidate is selected. Yet, many—both buyers and sellers—invest a good deal of time and psychic energy in a process that may not be very viable, that is a good deal less than it is said to be.

10

The Administrative Response

The financial constraints that the nation's colleges and universities have experienced in recent years have forced students to cope with fewer options and larger classes. One limited survey in 1992 reported that more colleges and universities than in an earlier study were simultaneously increasing the size of classes, reducing the number of full-time faculty, and increasing teaching loads. Class sizes were growing most rapidly in introductory and lower-division courses. There were no figures indicating how widespread these changes had become.

In addition to economies in the classroom, academic administrators have tried other ways to deal with the dollar gap. They have deferred maintenance and they have raised tuition and fees. A number of institutions report that they have been tightening budgets for some nonstudent-funded undergraduate activities. At the same time that they have been making savings in some areas, administrators have as a class greatly expanded their numbers, putting a new strain on institutional budgets.

One set of statistics shows that between 1975 and 1990, college and university enrollments rose 10 percent, the number of full-time faculty members increased 21 percent, and administrative positions grew 42 percent. On most campuses senior administrators are served by a growing number of minions called "associate," "vice," "deputy," "assistant," and "assistants to" in dealing with academic, research, administrative, graduate, student, athletic, public relations, development, business, or alumni matters.

To be sure, there is a greater need for more administrative involvement in record keeping, financial aid, fundraising, compliance with state and federal government regulations, and expanding student and faculty services. Faculty show little interest in taking on any of these tasks. Indeed, they constantly complain that, as it is, they are overburdened with administrative responsibilities. As a consequence of the growing demand for more middle-level administrative personnel, presently fewer than one-third of those employed in higher education are directly engaged in educating; two-thirds are administering or assisting those administering. There has clearly been a managerial revolution in higher education; there has been a unremitting increase in managers with growing influence.

According to the United States Equal Employment Opportunity Commission, staff changes at colleges and universities between 1975 and 1985 were as follows:

	1975	1985	Change (percent)
Total	1,388,406	1,577,087	13.6
Faculty (full-time)	446,830	473,537	5.9
Executive, administrative, and managerial	102,465	120,585	17.9
Other professionals	166,487	268,225	61.1
Service and maintenance	205,790	196,612	-4.9

The rapid and significant growth in nonteaching employees (the category "other professionals" includes, among others, financial aid counselors, auditors, coaches, and systems analysts) in institutions of higher learning in this ten-year period is so obvious it hardly needs comment. It is worth noting, however, that over the same period enrollment grew by 9.5 percent, so that in 1985 there were fewer full-time faculty per student in American institutions of higher learning than in 1975. The steady drift toward fewer full-time faculty per student has continued into the 1990s in both public and private institutions.

The trend in administrative bloat has been uninterrupted. There are, for example, more specialists involved in public relations and marketing. One study using more recent statistics shows that between 1985 and 1990, other professionals grew by 28 percent, executives by 14 percent, and faculty by less than 9 percent. Between 1985 and 1990, institutions of higher learning hired about twice as many nonteaching staff members as faculty members. In the 1980s, at some large research universities such as the University of Pennsylvania and Ohio State University, nonteaching professionals increased by over 100 percent. One cannot help but note the irony in the fact that at a time when colleges and universities were most loudly marketing themselves as institutions particularly committed to teaching, the proportion of employees who actually taught was steadily decreasing. The question that needs to be asked, of course, is: How much administrative growth was truly necessary during this period?

The point here is not simply the number of people, but, more importantly, costs. Since the 1920s, the proportion of college and university expenditures for administration have doubled. In every decade from 1930 to 1980 the growth in spending for administration outpaced the growth in spending for teaching. In the 1980s, administrative budgets grew 26 percent faster than instructional budgets.

In the 1930s, institutions of higher learning spent nineteen cents for administration for every dollar spent on instruction. By 1950, the figure was twenty-seven cents. In the 1987–88 academic year, it was forty-five cents. In the same year, the cost of administration (not including libraries, student services such as counseling, admissions or placement, expenditures for the physical plant, or outlays for research) was $1,742 per full-time student. [In contrast, in 1980 the cost of administration was only $1,189 (in 1988 dollars) per full-time student.]

According to figures reported in the *Digest of Educational Statistics,* between 1976–77 and 1990–91 for all types of institutions, with one exception, the percent of expenditures allotted to administrative functions increased while the percent allotted to instruction decreased:

Type of Institution	Percent Expenditures by Year			
	Administration		*Instruction*	
	1976–77	1990–91	1976–77	1990–91
Public universities	13.0	13.7	39.0	36.3
Public 4-year colleges	16.7	18.6	46.4	44.3
Public 2-year colleges	18.1	21.6	51.1	49.9
Private universities	13.2	14.8	38.0	38.3
Private colleges	20.4	22.2	37.3	33.4

According to another source, the College Board, from 1982 to 1992, administrative budgets increased by 26 percent at public institutions and by 45 percent at private institutions. During the same period, the proportion spent on instruction dropped from 32.4 percent to 30.7 percent. This unvarying upswing in administrative expenditures is in part due to outlays for administrative salaries. According to figures from the American Council on Education, between 1975 and 1985 faculty salaries in public institutions grew by a little more than 82 percent, while those of administrators (from presidents to financial aid directors) grew by about 89 percent. (In private institutions, the salary increases of administrators were only slightly greater than those of faculty.)

For example, at Purdue University, between 1982 and 1992 the total of salaries paid to the president and his thirteen vice presidents doubled, from $841,079 to $1,692,500. The president's salary went from $115,000 to $200,000. (This does not include, among other things, the free housing and credit card to charge travel and business expenses with which he is provided.) During this period, the salary of the vice president for physical facilities went from $58,000 to $112,600; that of the vice president for business services and assistant treasurer from $48,500 to $109,000; and that of the vice president for housing from $66,520 to $92,600. In addition to the president, half of the vice presidents were also provided with automobiles. At the same time, in the eight years between 1983–84 and 1991–92 the salary for full professors increased by 57.4 percent. The increase for associate professors was 51.3 percent, for assistant professors it was 53.6 percent, and for instructors it was 14.9 percent. Not only did the growth of administrators' salaries outpace that of faculty salaries, but their numbers also grew much more rapidly: between 1975 and 1989 the enrollment at Purdue increased 21 percent and the number of faculty rose 12 percent, while the number of administrative positions grew by 81 percent.

Moreover, at Purdue in 1992, all ten academic deans—agriculture, consumer and family sciences, education, engineering, liberal arts, management, nursing and health sciences, science, technology, and veterinary medicine—earned at least $100,000, from $106,000 to $149,800. All but two of the senior administrators had salaries in excess of $100,000, while only ninety-one, or less than 7 percent, of the faculty earned this much.[1]

A national survey of every private research university and highly ranked doctoral university, master's university and college, and liberal arts college (a total of over 400) found that in 1992–93 eight chief executives earned more than $400,000; ten more received at least $300,000 in salary, fees, bonuses, and benefits; sixty-seven were paid between $200,000 and $300,000; and the total salary and benefits for sixty-two others was between $175,000 and $200,000.[2]

Across the country administrative salaries have for years been higher than faculty salaries, and it is taken for granted that this is as it should be. In the last two decades the inequality has grown significantly. The consequence of this conjuncture is, among other things, an even steeper decline in the proportion of academic budgets available for rewarding efforts in teaching.

There are two obvious explanations for the striking growth of administrative salaries. First, some would contend that administrative salaries are market driven; that the skills, for example, leadership ability, necessary for staff work in colleges and universities, are truly out of the ordinary. There is a seller's market for academic administrators and their uncommon talents. They are in great demand. Any number of institutions of higher learning are eagerly waiting to recruit them. This external labor market for academic administrators drives up their salaries.

Although this interpretation may sound reasonable, it is not supported by fact. Indeed, research shows that the labor market forces that affect the salaries of academic administrators are relatively weak. There is not much of an external labor market competing for academic administrators. The majority spend their entire career in one or two institutions.[3] It is rare for them to find positions at an institution with more prestige than the one at which are located. About half move into their positions from within the same institution.[4]

Even those who move from one institution to another do not often do so through an open market. In spite of widespread advertising when a vacancy occurs, they are more often than not selected by a governing board, by a well-placed contact who is a senior administrator, or by a committee established and directed by institutional authorities who are less interested in an open search and the risk of in the end having to work with someone they do not want to work with than in knowing and trusting the successful candidate. One study found that after a national search only 24 percent of senior administrative positions were filled by individuals who applied directly, without any prior connection with the institution or the individuals doing the hiring. Moreover, close to half of the jobs and over half of the openings filled by those who did not directly respond to an advertisement went to individuals already at the employing institution.[5]

From their study of the careers of American college and university presidents, Cohen and March conclude that institutions of higher learning "typically engage in a national search for a new president and end up choosing someone who has a relatively close present or past connection with the school."[6] From this and other research the assertion that "higher education organizations are more likely to promote an insider to an administrative or professional position than to hire an external candidate" seems quite accurate, regardless of how systematic and extensive a canvass.[7]

On the other hand, princely administrative salaries can be understood as simple aggrandizement of college and university bureaucrats looking after themselves. Academic administrators are convinced that what they do is important and that it takes rare and special talent to do it. Top administrators who set salaries value those who perform similar tasks and who directly serve them, and see to it that they are amply rewarded.

In light of the disproportionate share of economic resources taken by them, it would not be unfair to fault academic administrators, at least in some part, for the situation in American colleges and universities with regard to teaching. The claim is heard that they are sympathetic about the putative imbalance in the reward structure in higher education. However, not only have they done little to address it, but their excessive claims on limited resources has clearly exacerbated the situation. It seems self evident: the more spent on administration, the less that can be spent on things other than administration.

Even as economic resources become scarcer, academic administrators still believe that they have first claim on them. As a particular example, in California in early 1994, after some politicians proposed a curb on spending for university executive leaves, the University of California president held what he assumed was a private video teleconference with his council of chancellors to make a proposal to circumvent the new policy. He was nearly successful, until his plan became public, and widespread indignation forced him to reverse his recommendation of $179,000 for a leave for the chancellor of the University of California at Santa Barbara, who was being pressured to resign. Just prior to the unfavorable publicity, the outgoing chancellor of the University of California at Davis was granted $155,000 for a terminal leave.

In sum, as a result of the managerial revolution on campus, administrators and administrative-related services have increased sharply, and there has been a professionalization of administrative functions. None of this has been conducive to setting right what teaching faculty see as inequities.

Academic administrators have been uncharacteristically resolute in their public pronouncements that more emphasis should be placed on classroom teaching and less on scholarly publications in assessing and rewarding college and university faculty. A good deal of this, of course, is mere posturing, but not always. Faculty that teach and only teach may not be more committed teachers, yet, with fewer disciplinary distractions, it is more likely that they will busy themselves with campus problems. It is generally believed that such activities ultimately benefit students.

To be sure, some faculty spend their time doing research because it is well understood that the pursuit of excellence and rewards in teaching is a fool's game. One must turn his or her attention to research or administrative chores if one is interested in following the smart money. Those who work hard at teaching and approach it with idealistic devotion are entrapped. If one's scholarship dwindles, one's marketplace value becomes nil. In effect, those whose sole focus is on teaching become hostages to the institution where they work. Academic administrators would have some interest in this eventuality. Having faculty engaged in teaching at the expense of disciplinary matters gives institutional authorities more control over them. One would expect faculty with fewer career options to be more compliant.

Notes

1. A. L. Starnes, "Administrative Growth Irritates Some Observers," and "Some Faculty View Administration as Bloated," *The Purdue Exponent* (13 April 1992): 1, 8–9, and (14 April 1992): 1, 8–9.
2. Douglas Lederman and Denise Magner, "What College Leaders Earn," *Chronicle of Higher Education* (14 September 1994): A25, A27–A43, A45.
3. Mary Ann D. Sagaria and Cynthia S. Dickens, "Thriving at Home: Developing a Career as an Insider," in Kathryn M. Moore and Susan B. Twombly (editors), *Administrative Careers and the Marketplace* [New Directions for Higher Education, No.72] (San Francisco: Jossey-Bass, 1990), 19.
4. Marlene Ross and Madeleine F. Green, "The Rules of the Game: The Unwritten Code of Career Mobility," in Moore and Twombly, *Administrative Careers and the Marketplace*, 70.
5. Daniel J. Socolow, "How Administrators Get Their Jobs," *Change* 10 (May 1978): 43.

6. Michael D. Cohen and James G. March, *Leadership and Ambiguity: The American College President* (New York: McGraw-Hill Book Company, 1974), 22.

7. Sagaria and Dickens, "Thriving at Home," 25.

11

Conclusions

Given much of the material reviewed to this point, one might precipitously conclude that it is somewhat surprising that those who teach at the college or university level put any effort into the enterprise. However, as a number of psychologists have for many years and often pointed out, all behavior is not controlled by external sources of reinforcement, by material rewards. There are activities that are intrinsically motivated, which absorb individuals and to which they are fully committed. Individuals engage in such activities largely to feel competent and self-determining. A person who is intrinsically motivated performs an activity for no apparent reason except the activity itself. This truth is generally lost sight of, and has been, since early in the century when Frederick W. Taylor convinced many that material rewards are necessary to ensure the maximum efforts of employees. Taylor's theory of scientific management assumes that employees are not self-motivated and need to be prodded with material rewards in order to be productive.

Whither the Motivation to Teach?

Clearly, for many academics, teaching is an intrinsically motivated activity. A good deal of what academics say about teaching would lead one to conclude that for many, it is an activity that is rewarding in itself. Many faculty, for whatever reason, enjoy teaching. It is a task that motivates, not because of the promise of some external reward, but because it is something they simply enjoy doing. Interesting and challenging students (given a great deal of academic freedom to develop interesting and challenging courses) can be rewarding to teaching faculty, certainly as rewarding as a salary increment or a teacher-of-the-year award. It is something that by itself gives value or pleasure, not the end toward which

147

it is directed. In sum, teaching in this case is not a means to an end, but an end in itself, something engaged in for its own sake. At the same time, it should not be forgotten that income has symbolic value, that it is a form of recognition. It denotes publicly and to its recipients responsibility and ability. It confers status.

One implication of all of this is that the rewards for working at teaching are mediated within an individual. Satisfaction need not come from extrinsic rewards, but can come from internal or affective sources such as positive emotional experiences. There are, of course, extrinsic rewards for being a college or university teacher, and these undoubtedly motivate individuals. Yet, it may be that these are not what primarily spark the many individuals who strive to perfect their teaching in the face of a great deal of evidence that, for the most part, students do not try very hard or learn very much. It would seem that there would be little justification to make any efforts at teaching if one considered only rewards, which were not or could not be affected, whatever faculty did in the classroom.

Although interdependent, intrinsic and extrinsic rewards are not additive. That is, the introduction of the latter sometimes produces shifts from the former, and vice versa. Indeed, there may be hidden and great costs in attempting to motivate faculty to become more committed teachers with the indiscriminate use of material rewards.

Psychologists have shown through many experiments that external controls, whether positive or negative, can undermine intrinsic motivation, particularly when they are used to control behavior.[1] Individuals may well discount intrinsic reasons for behavior if extrinsic reasons for it are present. When an extrinsic reward is added to intrinsically motivated behavior, the new, obvious external explanation can in effect decrease the intrinsic motivation for it. Thus, the relationship between intrinsic and extrinsic rewards can be negative. Deci has gone as far as to conclude that adding an extrinsic reward to an already intrinsically interesting task decreases the motivation for it.[2] After reviewing many studies, McGraw contends that creativity, thought, and resourcefulness (performance in general) are more likely to deteriorate when extrinsic rewards are introduced to motivate people. At the same time, intrinsically motivated people attend to and utilize information carefully, and are more careful, logical, and coherent in problem solving.[3] It would appear that extrinsic rewards cannot heedlessly be applied to intrinsically motivated activities, and if such rewards are made contingent on performance, the intrinsic motivation for the activity will decrease. Furthermore, other research has shown that when an extrinsic reward is modest, individuals reevaluate the intrinsic value of their behavior upward in order to justify it.[4] In short,

> studies suggest that one who is interested in developing and enhancing intrinsic motivation in children, employees, students, etc., should not concentrate on external-control systems such as monetary rewards, which are linked directly to performance, but, rather, he should concentrate on structuring situations that are intrinsically interesting and then be interpersonally supportive and rewarding toward the persons in the situation.[5]

It should be pointed out here that not all psychologists are convinced by the evidence at hand. Critiquing the question, Scott reminds us: "[I]t is altogether premature, if not meaningless, to assert that the administration of contingent monetary reinforcement will produce decrements in something called intrinsic motivation and behavior presumably determined by it."[6]

Surely, it would be fallacious to conclude that keeping faculty salaries low would motivate them to be better teachers. We know that individuals often will not put forth the effort and will not perform to capacity if they do not expect to be rewarded for it. Psychologists have found that those who feel underpaid do lessen their efforts. For example, Lord and Hohenfeld compared the performance of twenty-three major league baseball players who, because of contractual arrangements due to free agency, were paid lower salaries in the 1976 seasons than in 1975. On the whole, their performance in 1976 showed a marked drop off from the previous season (e.g., nonpitching players had lower batting averages, fewer home runs, and runs batted in), supporting the hypothesis that those who feel undercompensated will be less productive or perform less well.[7]

Although it is clear that the case has yet to be conclusively made, the weight of the evidence indicates that faculty motivated to teach simply as a result of salary increases and other extrinsic rewards are likely to feel that they are mere instruments, unfree, and as a consequence are less likely to value their teaching and any results it may produce. Still, there is little doubt that more thought and research is necessary before optimum strategies of how, in an unpromising academic labor market, faculty can be motivated to teach.

More on Salary Determination in Academia

The academic labor market is complicated and inelastic. Sellers occupy many niches, and they are not interchangeable. This is also the case with buyers.

Faculty are paid what the market they inhabit thinks they are worth. They get paid no more than it would cost to replace them. The market value for those with special abilities or unique characteristics rises because they cannot be readily replaced. Those who teach and do research are rarer than those who simply teach, and they get paid more. Pay differentials are due both to the qualities of those who perform various tasks and to the qualities of the various tasks that must be performed.

The market can deliver a teacher at a relatively low cost. A teacher who is a loyal servitor, for example, who helps with curriculum committees or who teaches a particularly popular course or who has given many years of service, has more local value than a teacher who is less visible. He or she will receive greater rewards, but they are limited as these activities have no national market.

Researchers cost more as research has a wider market than teaching, which only has local value. Because in the academic labor market information is imperfect, quality and value are not always traded at their true market value. Information costs and inefficiencies make it difficult for someone on another campus to figure out an individual's worth as a teacher. Information costs and inefficiencies have less effect on what is known about a researcher. A listing of publications or grant totals are more concrete than teaching reputation, and can readily be obtained. And those who do research can deliver teaching as a by-product. To be sure, across-the-board salary increment policies and union contracts act to cushion the full effects of the academic labor market.

Status competition and the pursuit of money leads institutions of higher learning to compete for faculty and students. Faculty who have interests in addition to teaching are less likely to be overbearing pedants who too closely monitor the academic achievements of students. As a consequence, they are less likely to cause student distress and pain. Certainly the majority of students are not fully committed to their studies, and even if they were, they would prefer to avoid either or both. Distress and pain can lead to high student attrition, a condition academic administrators would prefer to avoid. High drop out rates and declining enrollments can anger parents, governing boards, the public, and politicians.

Not only is it generally the case that there are fewer openings for faculty than candidates to fill them, but there are more openings for students than applicants to fill them. Because of the shortage of undergraduates, colleges and universities are faced with the perennial problem of bolstering enrollments. This is primarily done by keeping academic standards relatively low, by providing abundant extra-curricular activities, and by subsidizing educational costs. It is hardly surprising that students are undercharged and faculty are underpaid. Since the founding of the American college it has been assumed that through altruism and substandard remuneration faculty could be depended on to be a reliable benefactor to underfunded higher education.

Some Final Thoughts

To a limited extent, academic salaries are set by supply and demand. As David Ricardo recognized over 175 years ago, "labor is dear when it is scarce and cheap when it is plentiful." The arguments used to justify more economic rewards for efforts in the classroom are not grounded in social science theory, but are basically ethical: proponents contend that teaching should be more generously rewarded because it is right and proper or fair and just. However, this might not be easily done. As one extensive and widely read examination of the distribution of earnings concludes: "We have found that the main cause of the inequality of pay is the inequality of abilities to work. There are great difficulties in the way of breaking the link between pay and ability, and prescribing equal pay for unequal work. The best way to reduce the inequality of the effect is to reduce that of the cause."[8] And one additional fact needs to be restated here: the demand for teachers and teaching is not high, not as high as it is for those who teach and do research. If the remuneration for those who only teach and those who teach and do research were made more comparable, then the supply and demand would be thrown out of balance, and fewer academics would spend time doing research.

Students may want to learn job-related skills and they may want to work for good grades; they also may want their undergraduate years to be successful and happy. But there is not a great deal of evidence that they want to learn very much beyond what is needed to graduate or to get a job, that they want all that their teachers can give them. Few undergraduates are truly interested in what faculty study or teach: they learn next to nothing, forget most of that, and are hardly changed by the college experience. A significant number are simply indifferent about their education. When students skip out of classes that they are not required to attend—particularly large lecture courses with enrollments of 200 or more—it is too readily assumed that this is a natural reaction to a boring, impersonal, or alienating experience. It could also mean that they are lazy, preoccupied with other matters (jobs, family life, friendships, the pursuit of leisure, etc.) and hope to get by with the minimum amount of effort.

Quite simply, there is no evidence that the quality of teaching is an important factor in determining whether or not students stay in or leave college. Obviously, they would prefer a pleasant experience when attending a lecture, but this does not mean that they care about being taught, whether it is important if the teaching is good or bad. When asked about college, their classroom experiences are not something that come immediately to their minds. In one of the most comprehensive studies of whether "college makes a difference," the authors note:

> When we asked our students why they are in college, the answer is, overwhelmingly, "to get a degree to get a job." Unlike graduation-day speakers, they seldom mention cultivating the intellect, becoming active citizens, enriching the mind and spirit, or developing character.... Most students are quite utilitarian about their education; that is, they evince a strong interest in instrumental career success.[9]

Given what students get from their undergraduate years, there is no way to determine (or is it necessary in most cases to determine) if colleges or universities are doing a good job. There is no way of knowing if teaching were assessed better and effort and outcome more adequately rewarded students would get a better education. One cannot conclude that if quality of teaching and rewards were more closely related academic life would be better. Thus, there is little reason to change the distribution of rewards in colleges and universities if the goal is primarily to improve the education of undergraduates.

The proportionality rule of distributive justice as set down by Aristotle would not lead one to conclude that relative to other activities of college and university faculty the rewards for teaching should be greater. According to the proportionality rule, those who have contributed more of a given good or who have contributed a more valuable good should receive more in return. The most valuable goods are those—such as the products of research—that are in short supply relative to demand. In light of the case that has been made for what teaching does or fails to do, the argument that faculty who contribute to academic life largely through teaching are not receiving their due is not compelling.

The fact that considerations other than those that are simply materialistic motivate some portion of the professoriate bears repeating. In light of academic culture, we do not even know to what degree increasing extrinsic rewards would increase the motivation of academics. That is, we do not know that if teachers were offered more money to work harder and teach better they would work harder and teach better, or if teachers were in some way punished for not teaching well they would be motivated to do better. There may well be some difference in how those giving rewards or punishments and those receiving them interpret a situation. For example, punishment may lessen efforts rather than increase them. Given such considerations, it is difficult to calculate the effects on faculty motivation of limited institutional rewards combined with very limited opportunities for mobility by virtue of exclusion from the academic labor market. Surely it is doubtful whether they would be positive.

At the same time, it is worth noting that the survey of mathematicians referred to at the end of chapter 7 "found no evidence that the teaching was more effective in those departments that paid more attention to rewarding teaching than in those that did not. What we found was that faculty felt that teaching deserved a higher status in the reward structure than it had."[10]

The consequence of the disparity in how the academic labor market works, how it is thought to work, and how it is thought it should work is a chronically frustrated professoriate, a pervasive feeling of not being fully appreciated and of not being fairly rewarded for efforts and contributions. The barbed attacks by vocal critics and media-spread contention that compared to scholars and scientists teaching faculty are exploited feeds the discontent. Teaching faculty are encouraged in thinking themselves cheated by life. Many who have the time to publish are aware that as matters stand the returns for their efforts are also modest, and this may, in part, explain why the output of those who seem to have so much promise is so meager. The fact that those in most other occupations have fared far worse is of small consolation. Surely a sense of achievement is necessary to motivate people. As

Elliot Liebow has observed, "no man can live with the terrible knowledge that he is not needed."

> By itself, then, work alone does not guarantee full and valued participation in society. Participation requires not only an opportunity to contribute to the day-to-day life of that society, but it requires, reciprocally, an acknowledgment by society that the contribution is of value. That acknowledgment, typically in the form of wages, lets the man know that he is somebody, that he is important, useful and even necessary.[11]

The willingness to work increases for those who feel that their efforts are seen by others as valuable and are appreciated. As Liebow points out, one indication that what one does is seen as valuable (or significant) is for it to be appropriately rewarded, or at least in some way recognized.

The academic marketplace operates in such a way that teaching is at most a marginal consideration in the assessment of individuals; one is as likely to be rewarded for one's pedigree or for the prestige (earned or unearned) one brings to a campus. If the neoclassical labor market model worked as expected the relative salaries of faculty who teach and only teach should increase if the demand for teaching and teachers increased (which could be done by limiting class size or the output of Ph.D.s). Of course, the neoclassical labor market model does not always work as expected. If it did, given anticipated rewards, institutions would pay to train teachers and individuals would pay to be trained as researchers and academic administrators.

Other propositions of economics would also suggest why teaching is not more highly rewarded. The productivity or contribution of a college or university teacher is not easy to measure; it is difficult, if not impossible, to demonstrate effective teaching. Number of students taught certainly indicates little, and it is not an easy matter to assess what students learn (if anything). Thus, the remuneration of faculty is in part determined by what they could earn elsewhere—what economists call opportunity wage. This idea can be used to explain why computer scientists earn more than literary scholars, but it can also explain why those who engage in activities in addition to teaching have a wider range of employment opportunities and can expect higher salaries. The point that only a small minority of faculty publish on a regular bases and rewards—which are always scarce—would almost inescapably go to this seemingly special few seems fairly obvious and needs to be reiterated.

Further, it is an article of faith that those who contribute most to an institution should and do earn more. Since institutions of higher learning trade, in part, in prestige, and those who do research contribute more to this than those who only teach, it would be expected that they would be seen as contributing more (as would those who spend their time at administrative activities) and would be rewarded accordingly. In addition, and not to be overlooked, researchers who sometimes bring large grants to campus also have special value which many believe is deserving of some recompense.

Many academics believe that their leveled career trajectory is due to a passing buyer's market. But it is clear that there is a more overriding reason—namely, that they are teachers—why they are shut out of the academic marketplace. The facts suggest that, regardless of what efforts or seeming success faculty may have in the classroom, they cannot expect that the academic labor market will bring about conditions that will enhance their rewards.

More often than not—and certainly in recent years—the academic labor market can be characterized as a buyer's market. In addition, resources within institutions have been generally scarce. In spite of all the handwringing by those whose actions might be able to effect some change, academic administrators, faculty with the most commitment and who put forth the most effort in carrying out their teaching responsibilities, are not rewarded for this. It has been true in academia for years that those with the heaviest teaching loads earn the lowest salaries,[12] as salaries are generally higher in top-tier schools than in lower-tier schools.

The positive relationship between low status and heavy teaching load perfectly exemplifies the Matthew Effect—to he who hath, shall be given. Not only do less prestigious institutions have the heaviest teaching loads, but within an institution faculty with the lowest prestige (or rank) have the most contact hours with undergraduates. And the heavier one's teaching load, the more difficult it is to enhance one's status through the publication of articles or books and the receipt of research grants.

There are few favorable signs from the academic labor market to motivate faculty. If some faculty lack motivation, it is not surprising. It is curious that more attention is not given to the interests of the faculty in setting institutional priorities and distributing rewards in light of the pioneering Western Electric Hawthorne study and a great deal of research since then that leads to the inevitable conclusion that maximum productivity can be achieved if the needs and desires of employees are given primary consideration. To the degree that a tenet of economic theory that greater rewards elicit greater effort is correct, then it is obvious that academic administrators could with minimal monetary incentives at least marginally affect the quality of teaching on American campuses. All academic administrators seem to do is publicly and loudly bemoan the cruel fate of teaching faculty. This, of course, only adds to their disgruntlement. If academic administrators have no inclination or cannot truly make the life of teaching faculty better, it would perhaps be best if they would forgo the banalities.

There is an elemental truth that has been overlooked by all parties involved in the debate regarding the appropriate rewards for those who teach. This is that if the role of the professor is to involve something more than merely being a school teacher, he or she has a responsibility to enlarge the knowledge of his or her discipline. It is not a compelling argument to contend that it is impossible for all academics to do research because too many have excessive teaching loads. If this is the case, then teaching loads for those whose classroom responsibilities preclude engaging in scholarship or science should be reduced to give them the time to do so. Moreover, the problem need not be one of inadequate facilities. As Kirkland put it nearly fifty years ago: "As long as motor cars and trains run, cyclotrons and observatories are not campus prerequisites for research in science, nor a library of four million volumes for the historian or the sociologist."[13] An institution that took steps—such as reducing teaching loads—that permitted all faculty to do research would not be making the job of the professoriate easier; it and its students would be the beneficiaries:

> The college that wishes to develop a responsible faculty must value the ritual of scholarship. It must do more. It should neither burden its teachers with excessive schedules nor follow a policy of ca'canny with leaves and sabbaticals. When an institution, following such short-sighted policies, complains of the irresponsibility of a faculty member, the responsibility for that irresponsibility often lies in the decisions of administrators or the proceedings of trustees.[14]

This seems self-evident. It clearly makes more sense than the oft-heard contention that the definition of scholarship should be broadened to include teaching (or the preparation for teaching). This would have no effect on the academic labor market.

As matters presently stand, it is clear that most faculty members cannot depend on extrinsic incentives to motivate them. The belief on the part of many that they in some way change students might help keep them going. The unrelenting stream of rhetoric and cant by self-proclaimed and media-appointed spokespersons for colleges and universities may also motivate those who believe that those who appear to be in a position to change things truly care about them. The fact of the matter, however, is that those who value idle curiosity and the life of the mind are the least in need of external rewards to motivate them.

Notes

1. Edward L. Deci, *Intrinsic Motivation* (New York and London: Plenum Press, 1975).
2. Edward L. Deci, "Effects of Externally Mediated Rewards on Intrinsic Motivation," *Journal of Personality and Social Psychology* 18 (April 1971): 105-15.
3. Kenneth O. McGraw, "The Detrimental Effects of Reward on Performance: A Literature Review and a Prediction Model," in Mark R. Lepper and David Greene (eds.), *The Hidden Costs of Reward: New Perspectives on the Psychology of Human Motivation* (Hillsdale, N.J.: Erlbaum, 1978), 33-60.
4. Leon Festinger and James M. Carlsmith, "Cognitive Consequences of Forced Compliance," *Journal of Abnormal and Social Psychology* 58 (March 1959): 203-10.
5. Edward L. Deci, "Intrinsic Motivation, Extrinsic Reinforcement, and Inequity," *Journal of Personality and Social Psychology* 22 (April 1972): 119-20.
6. W. E. Scott, Jr., "The Effects of Extrinsic Rewards on 'Intrinsic Motivation': A Critique," *Organizational Behavior and Human Performance* 15 (February 1976): 128.
7. Robert G. Lord and Jeffrey A. Hohenfeld, "Longitudinal Field Assessment of Equity Effects on the Performance of Major League Baseball Players," *Journal of Applied Psychology* 64 (February 1979): 19-26. [It should be pointed out that further research on this question with a larger sample does not fully support the equity theory predictions of decrements in performance. See Dennis Duchon and Arthur G. Jago, "Equity and the Performance of Major League Baseball Players: An Extension of Lord and Hohenfeld," *Journal of Applied Psychology* 66 (December 1981): 728-32.]
8. Henry Phelps Brown, *The Inequality of Pay* (Berkeley and Los Angeles: University of California Press, 1977), 332.
9. William E. Knox, Paul Lindsay, and Mary N. Kolb, *Does College Make a Difference?: Long-Term Changes in Activities and Attitudes* (Westport, Conn.: Greenwood Press, 1993), xviii-xix.
10. *Recognition and Rewards in the Mathematical Sciences,* Report of the Joint Policy Board for Mathematics, Committee on Professional Recognition and Rewards (Washington, D.C.: American Mathematical Society, 1994), 7.
11. Elliot Liebow, "No Man Can Live with the Terrible Knowledge That He Is Not Needed," *New York Times Magazine* (5 April 1970): 28-29, 129ff. Sociological research generally supports this point. More recently, for example, Duneier has written: "Human beings desire to participate in a world that validates their own

image of self-worth." Mitchell Duneier, *Slim's Table* (Chicago: University of Chicago Press, 1992), 109.

12. "How Devalued Is Teaching?" *Newsletter* (University Park, Pa.: National Center on Postsecondary Teaching, Learning, & Assessment) 2, (Winter 1993): 1.

13. Edward C. Kirkland, "Recipe for Responsibility," *American Association of University Professors Bulletin* 34 (Spring 1948): 24.

14. Ibid.

Index